"If you want to teach adults successfully and enjoyably, this is the book to have at hand."

Ronald Gross, author of *The Lifelong Learner*

"A marvelously comprehensive and practical guide to teaching adults. Useful for frequent reference."

Allen Tough, author of *The Adults Learning Projects*

"A down-to-earth book dealing with reality. There are many specifics that will be helpful to the experienced practitioner as well as to the beginner."

Leonard Nadler, author of *Developing Human Resources*

"A book which is useful to all adult education teachers-beginning and experienced. Draves writes in a very readable style with jargon-free language."

Donald W. Mocker, in *The Adult Learning Review of Books*

HOW TO
T E A C H
A D U L T S

WILLIAM A. DRAVES

Fourth Edition

Published by LERN Books, a division of the Learning Resources Network (LERN), P.O. Box 9, River Falls, Wisconsin 54022, U.S.A.

Library of Congress Cataloging in Publication Data
Draves, William A., 1949-
    How To Teach Adults, fourth edition

Bibliography: p.
1. Adult education. LC5215.D73   1984
ISBN: 1-57722-034-X

Manufactured in the United States of America
    7   6   5   4   3   2

"Information That Works!"

Preface to the Fourth Edition

Since the first edition was published, the popularity of *How To Teach Adults* has been continuous and steady. Sales have topped 100,000. The book has been translated into Japanese. Institutions have ordered hundreds of copies of *How To Teach Adults* for all their teachers. People in all walks of life use the book, from instructors of professional training courses, to those doing avocational and leisure-learning subjects. Within the genre of books on the teaching of adults, this book has continued to maintain its relevance and its place as one of the crucial texts of the genre.

While the author professes only to be a good teacher among equals, it is the continuing praise for the book from teachers that is most gratifying.

The fourth edition consists of updates, revisions and additions. It also contains two more significant additions. First, in this edition we predict and plan for every in-person course to become a hybrid course. As a result, in this edition, we integrate tips and techniques for incorporating online learning and teaching features into traditional face-to-face courses. Second, improving completion rates in higher education is now an urgent issue of crucial importance, along with the reality that most college students are now non-traditional students. Thus, there is a new section on Teaching Adults in Higher Education for those of you who are teaching in higher education.

The new edition neither negates nor neglects anything of substance in the first three editions. The successful practices and techniques remain the same; the act of teaching continues to be a mixture of some basic principles and how-to techniques, and there is still no one best way to teach adults. Luckily for all of us, there is still room and necessity for "the art of teaching," for creativity, for individuality, for the uniqueness of you as a teacher in the company of your learners to make learning a joyous, wonderful experience.

Acknowledgments

As a journalist in adult learning, I am indebted first to those who have made this story: teachers, past and present; including those who have taught me and those I interviewed for this book.

Those who have written before me include mid-century great masters, such as J.R. Kidd and Gilbert Highet. And there are those more recent great masters whom it has been my privilege and honor to know personally, such as Malcolm Knowles and Jerry Apps.

And there are my equals, thousands of other teachers from whom I have learned much.

Finally, I want to thank Julie Coates for her support and her example of a teacher without equal.

How to Teach Adults

Chapter 1.
Introduction

One day, Karen Thiel was teaching her Life Work Planning class at the technical institute in Fond du Lac, Wisconsin. In the middle of the class, a woman mistakenly walked into her class room. Instead of leaving, the woman was captivated by the exercises the class was doing, and joined in.

At the end of the class, the woman told Mrs. Thiel, "It's been very fascinating, and very enjoyable, but next week I'm going to *have* to go to my creative writing class."

You too can teach a class so interesting that even a person who is supposed to be somewhere else will find it exciting.

This book will help you teach adults in a group or classroom setting. It was written to provide you with proven techniques for preparing, conducting, and improving your class. You may be new to teaching adults, and see this as an introduction to lifelong learning. Or you may have taught adults before, and want to continue learning by incorporating new ideas.

As you read this book, you will gain new insights into helping adults learn, pick up tips on different learning techniques, and be able to evaluate your experience better. In doing so, you will make your teaching more stimulating.

A Different Kind of Teacher

Welcome to the learning explosion. People are interested in learning just about anything these days, from practical skills like home repair to philosophical issues about life after death. The range of topics is unlimited, from the outer reaches of the universe to the inner workings of the brain. We are now in a world in which a person can study just about any imaginable topic.

No longer are people content to sit back and say, "I have my education," but instead are making learning a lifelong pursuit. This has meant a new era for teaching as well, with different approaches and techniques for helping adults learn. It has called for a different kind of teacher, one who understands how adults learn, one who can create a positive climate for learning, one who can tap the experiences and talents of the students themselves, and one who is a lifelong learner and wants to improve his own facilitating of adult learning.

In fact, in this new era, adult learning is no longer limited to adults. Rather, an "adult learner" is one who chooses to be in a given learning situation. Thus, the term "adult learners" refers to people of all ages, including teenagers and even children when they voluntarily participate in a group learning activity or class.

To respond to the needs of today's adult learner, thousands of people who have never taught before are doing so. Their entrance into teaching is not as teachers but as people with a particular skill or knowledge of a subject they want to share. Some of these new teachers, teaching part-time for relatively modest reimbursement, do not even think of themselves as teachers. They are joined by professional teachers and trainers - people who have been trained to teach for a living, but for whom teaching adults is somewhat different from previous formal instruction. They all have in common the desire to share what they know with others.

We want to teach because we have a need to share knowledge. There are two reasons for this. First, we know more now. Every person has a wealth of information and skills to offer others. And secondly, teaching is one of the best avenues or ways to tutor or help others. In past decades, we passed on ideas though the family, the church, civic groups, and other organizations. Today, teaching is a primary channel for conveying knowledge. Consequently, the opportunity to share one's own knowledge with other adults in a class setting is an inviting one for many people like you.

The tradition of people teaching other people is long. Although professional teachers have always had a place in our society, we tend to forget that lay teaching has a rich history as well. One hundred years ago, there were fewer colleges as compared with today. Yet people learned, and they learned from each other. Fathers taught their sons a trade; mothers taught their daughters homemaking skills. Skilled laborers took on apprentices. In addition, there were libraries, lyceums, chautauquas, Extension, and other places to teach adults. Later, adults taught others in Sunday school, as scout leaders, in civic organizations, and in professional associations. Our opportunity to teach and the knowledge we possess about teaching adults have grown out of those traditions of adults teaching adults.

This new learning explosion is occurring predominantly in the class or group setting - two or more people led by a facilitator or teacher. Within that common format, the learning is varied in its location, subject, and sponsorship. It is taking place in formal class rooms, in living rooms, in work places and offices, in large lecture halls, in parks, and even in restaurants and taverns. Most of these classes are not for credit or certification; some are for credits, continuing education units, or certificates; but all are taking place because adults want to learn.

All kinds of organizations are participating: colleges and universities, community colleges and technical institutes; public schools; city recreation agencies; learning networks; employers, businesses and corporations; civic, community and voluntary organizations; associations; social agencies, mental health centers, hospitals; and independent centers. In addition, many unaffiliated individuals are offering courses independently.

Why You Should Read This Book

Why should you read part or all of this book? Because teaching adults is difficult, and the learning situation is fragile. The importance of knowing the information in this book is critical. It can make the difference between a successful class and an unsuccessful one.

The chapters of the book show you how to plan better, teach, and improve your class. They will also show you how to turn teaching from a chore into a joy. You can help others learn, and that is one of life's more rewarding experiences. Wherever you are teaching, you can turn the classroom or living room into a learning room. If you are enthusiastic, your students will have fun learning and learn more.

Little things can turn teaching from a chore into a joy. Just changing the title of the course altered the attitude of Reeta Grover, a Columbus, Ohio policewoman who had to teach a course on careers for women in public safety. When administrator Margaret Anschild helped her reword the course title from "Women in Police Careers" to "It's Not a Crime to Apply," Officer Grover remarked, "This changed my whole outlook. Now I'm looking forward to teaching the course."

You may want to read the whole book, skim it, or read those parts most useful to you. Basically, three aspects are covered in the book. The first is how adults learn and how you can help them learn better. The second is how to prepare for your class. The third contains various tips and ideas for teaching and improving your teaching techniques.

Almost all of the suggestions come not from the author, but from the deep and varied experiences of teachers, learners, and educators over a long period of time. They have been culled from other books, from articles, from personal conversations, and from actual class sessions to make this a book of commonly understood principles about teaching adults.

An Invitation to Teach

This is your invitation to teach - to join in one of the more important functions in life, passing on knowledge and skills to others. It is an activity that has taken place in doorways and on street corners, in academies and under marble columns, from Socrates to modern-day teachers, media commentators, independent scholars, and those who teach by doing.

Teaching is both an opportunity and a responsibility. It is an opportunity for you to grow, to learn more, to gain a valuable skill that will help you in your work, career advancement, ability to relate to others, self-esteem, and feeling of worth. It is an opportunity to meet and enjoy people. But it is also a responsibility to your learners to create the kind of climate in which they will feel comfortable, secure, and able to learn. You are charged with demonstrating to them that you know they are not there to hear you pontificate or soak up your words of wisdom, but to internalize and be responsible for their own learning. Your duty is not so much to teach as to help them learn. You are to help them achieve whatever goal they have set for themselves and to foster additional learning.

Part I.
How We Learn

Chapter 2.
How Adults Learn

*"A teacher must be a learner himself. If he has lost
his capacity for learning, he is not good enough to be in
the company of those who have preserved theirs."*

— Harry Overstreet, early 20th Century adult educator

When twelve people walk into your class for the first time, each one will come already equipped with various experiences, attitudes, perceptions, and ideas. Each person will organize his or her thoughts differently, and each will be able to absorb new knowledge and ideas in his or her own way.

The adult's mental learning state is not a blank chalkboard on which you, the teacher, can write as you wish. Neither is the adult learner's head an empty pail for you to fill with your knowledge and ideas. The adult learner's chalkboard already has many messages on it, and his mental pail is almost full already. Your job as teacher is not to fill a *tabula rasa*, but to help your participants reorganize their own thoughts and skills. A prerequisite to helping adults learn is to understand how they learn.

As complex human beings, we bring to the learning situation a combined set of emotional, physical, mental, and social characteristics that make each one of us unique. The way to approach this diversity in learners is with variety in your teaching. To do that, it is best to understand some of the characteristics of adults.

Emotional Characteristics

Adults' emotional states are inextricably tied up in their ability to learn. To learn, an adult must be emotionally comfortable with the learning situation. Indeed, some educators have gone so far as to equate a good emotional state with learning. Says J. Roby Kidd in *How Adults Learn*, "Feelings are not just aids or inhibitors to learning; the goal of learning and of emotional development are parallel and sometimes identical and can probably be most conveniently stated as self-realization and self-mastery."[1]

Throughout the ages, one's emotional state has always been manipulated to try to induce learning, but somehow the attempt to produce positive feelings became distorted in the mistaken belief that greater learning would occur if one produced negative feelings of pain, fear, or anxiety.

The dunce cap, a sign of humiliation, was not originally intended to be so. Instead, the cone-shaped headgear was believed to have magical powers, just as some contemporaries believe the similar pyramid shape has unknown powers. Putting the cap on one who had missed a question or needed help was not a punishment, but was believed to help that person learn. Over the years, the symbolism changed from a positive helping gesture to a sign of humiliation and ignorance.

Unfortunately, vestiges of the punishment principle either consciously or unconsciously are present in even the most enlightened classes. Learning can be inhibited by frowns and other gestures.

In helping a person learn, the teacher must be able to help create a positive emotional climate, and the key to that state is the learner's *self-image*.

Although most adults come to class mentally ready to learn, at the same time, they may be inhibited from learning by a poor self image. That poor self-concept may not be correct, may not be rational, but nevertheless exists in many people. It comes from various sources.

A shy person may feel unable to participate to meet the expectations of others in the class. A manager who has been turned down for several promotions may feel trapped in a dead-end job and doubt the value of learning anything. A housewife who has stayed at home with children for many years may feel she is not current or informed enough to converse on an adult level again. Someone who has been out of school for several decades may feel incapable of studying anymore, and may fear being left far behind the other students. The causes of a less-than-sensitive self-image are many. They stem from natural feelings about inadequacy and growing older, and some are induced artificially by society.

Physical Characteristics

Abraham Lincoln may have been able to read at night by fire light, and children may have learned in straight-backed wooden desks in drafty log cabin schools, but today's adults can detect and be influenced by the slightest changes in comfort. Adults are more attuned to comfortable surroundings, more sensitive to discomfort.

Our physical state affects our capacity to learn. Physique and intelligence are related because our bodies influence how and whether we can learn.

Room temperature. Try to make your setting comfortable, neither too warm nor too cold. Older people chill more easily, and your sense of warmth may not coincide with those in your group. In a small crowded room, your participants will become hot and stuffy sitting next to each other sooner than you will. Ask your participants to tell you if they are uncomfortable. If you have little control over the room's temperature, encourage your participants to wear layered clothing.

Vision. To compensate for visual difficulties of learners of all ages, think carefully about how you can make words, charts, objects, even yourself, clear to all your participants.

Set up your room so that no one has to look directly into sun light. Make sure there is enough overhead lighting. If you use a flip chart, use large letters when writing on it. Seat people so they can see each other. Participants will engage in discussion and learn more from each other if they can see each other.

Hearing. Just as important as seeing well is hearing well. Inability to hear well, either because of one's own capability or because of the setting, can make learners feel insecure, less intelligent, isolated, and far less willing to participate.

In preparing your class, think about how you can ensure that every participant will hear you. Try to select a room that is reasonably free of outside street noises, or noises from other rooms in the same building. Listen for any interference from heating sources, air conditioning, coffee pots, and any other systems or appliances in the room.

Design your space so that you can always be heard by your participants, and so that they can hear each other. If you have a large class, experiment to see if a microphone helps or hinders. Speak in clear, loud, and distinct tones. Don't talk to your group with your back turned to them while you are concentrating on something else, like setting up some projection equipment. Ask as often as you need to whether people in the back can hear you. When others in the class are talking, make sure they are facing the majority of the class. Ask people to stand up if necessary. Repeat questions from the group so everyone can hear them.

Mental Characteristics

Although adults may come to the learning situation with bodies that are not always in prime shape, the story is different for their mental attitudes. Mentally, adults are eager to learn.

Several aspects of adult learning mentality relate to your helping them to learn: a readiness to learn, problem orientation, and time perspective.

A readiness to learn. Adults for the most part will come to your class ready to learn. Almost all adult learning is voluntary these days, and even societal coercion, such as peer pressure, does not seem to affect adult learners. They attend because they want to.

Part of that readiness may be a natural growth process in which "true learning" - self-study, personal inquiry, or self-directed learning- is more welcome after one's formal schooling or education ends. Even the sixteenth century master of self-study, Montaigne, wrote about his education, "At thirteen ... I had completed my course, and in truth, without any benefit that I can now take into account."[2] Whether their experiences in school were beneficial or not so positive, adults want to view their adult learning experiences as separate from more formal school, and will approach them differently. This may be because adults are not only ready to learn but need to learn.

Problem orientation. Education for children is often subject centered, concentrating on various disciplines like philosophy and science, and the abstract as well as the practical. Adult learning, on the other hand, is more problem-centered. Adults want to learn to solve or address a particular problem, and are more satisfied with their learning if it applies to everyday

10

experiences, is practical, or is current.

Adults are oriented toward problem solving because they are faced with certain developmental tasks stemming from the roles they assume, or want to assume, in their families, work, and society. These tasks and roles demand a good deal of adjustment, accomplishment, and learning. Although society pushes few adults into the classroom, it certainly creates enough needs and wants to encourage adults to perform their best in various roles and life stages.

Time perspective. Another and related impetus for problem orientation in adult learning is that an adult's time perspective is different from that of a child. For a child, time, both past and future, is a vast quantity. A year ago is a long time, and the future is endless. Increasingly, as one becomes older, time becomes less expendable and more limited. The future is not so endless after all, and the past blurs a little so that ten years wasn't all that long ago. As time becomes more limited, it becomes more important. In the learning situation, adults prefer what can be learned today or in the near future to what can be learned over a longer period of time.

The adult's interest in solving problems within their older time perspective makes adults more concerned with specific narrow topics of relevance than broad, generalized or abstract subjects.

A readiness to learn, problem orientation, and specific time perspective contribute to an internal motivation to learn.

The time and problem orientations do not imply that everything adults want to learn is so immediate as fixing the plumbing. Many different kinds of issues, thoughts, and ideas may constitute a timely problem. For one person, finding out whether beauty lies in a musemn painting or in a mountaintop view may constitute a legitimate learning problem. For another person, determining how the ancient philosophers combined work with study may be an equally immediate problem.

Social Characteristics

The most important social characteristic of the adult learner is an abundance and variety of *experiences*. This aspect alone makes teaching adults different from teaching children or youth.

Your participants will be coming from different backgrounds, occupations,

11

types of upbringing, ethnic heritages, and parts of town. Each one will have a different mix of experiences and previously formed perceptions when entering your class. Some of these perceptions are about school group interactions and about the subject.

School. Even if you are not working in a school-like atmosphere, structured learning situations are inevitably associated with previous schooling. For many people, their formal schooling was less than successful. Many adults received low grades in school and have some stigma attached to that period of time. Others may have outwardly done well in school, but inwardly felt the experience was boring or a waste of time. Generally speaking, it is best to reduce the number of associations with formal schooling in your references, style, and approach to your subject. When teaching those with unfavorable school experiences, it is wise not to repeat those mannerisms and actions which may remind your participants of their past situations. The imprint of our schooling is still on all of us, and if those memories are not good, it is best not to revive them.

Group interactions. Your class is just one kind of group in which adults participate. Some will come with positive expectations about interacting in a group; some will not. Some will come wanting to be leaders in the group; others will have already decided before the class starts to be passive or take a minimal role in group participation. Some will see the group as an opportunity to display talent and knowledge while others will see it as a possible threat to exposing their lack of talent and knowledge.

The subject. Every adult coming to your class will have some perception about the subject to be discussed. Some will have a degree of proficiency in the topic; others will have been acquainted more superficially. Some will have had a negative encounter with the topic, or gained some misinformation. Others will have thought about it from a distance, but come with curiosity and some ideas not based on reality, but on what others have said or done.

Social psychologist Gardner Murphy says that adults, contrary to common assumption, are not able to detach themselves emotionally from the subject at hand. "The adult has not fewer but more emotional associations with factual material than do children, although we usually assume that he has less," he says.[3]

Working with your participants' experiences is perhaps your most rewarding challenge. These varied and copious experiences need to be

12

handled on two levels. First, you as a teacher need to deal with the backgrounds your participants bring to class. If someone has a negative image of schooling, you may have to help that person see this situation as different from past schooling. If a person in the group has gained some misinformation about the subject, you will need to clarify how they were misinformed. If some of your participants automatically shy away from participating in a group, you may want to try to draw them out or structure exercises to give them as much interaction as your over-eager students have.

On another level, you have an abundant resource at hand in the past experiences of class members. Each has some event, skill, idea, or knowledge worth sharing with the rest of the group. As Sharon Merriam and Rosemary Cafarella note, "Life experience functions in several ways ... Adults call upon their past experiences in the formulation of learning activities, as well as serving as one another's resources in a learning event."[4] You can tap into the variety of backgrounds to illustrate your points, to encourage discussion, to stimulate peer teaching, and to gain new knowledge yourself. It is this wealth in your participants that makes teaching adults so exciting and rewarding. Drawing on your participants' experiences can make the class an exciting and new interaction every time you teach; to ignore the past is to miss out on something valuable and special.

The Brain and Learning

"Many teachers probably believe that the function of the brain is to learn algebra or to learn how to diagram sentences, or to be able to read and interpret great literature," notes Julie Coates in *Education in the 21st Century*[5]. "Indeed," she says, "our brains are capable of all these tasks, but that is not why we have a brain. We have a brain for only one purpose, and that purpose is survival. The function of the brain is to allow us, as living beings, to understand and respond to our environment in ways that will assure that we survive and propagate our species."

Because our brain's top priority is keeping us alive, there are certain functions that have evolved over the thousands of years of our existence, and which are "hard-wired" in our neurological functioning. They are responses and reactions to the environment that occur when we find ourselves in certain types of situations. Certain parts of the brain can, and do, change fairly rapidly in response to a new environment, such as the Internet. However, other parts of the brain still basically function as they have over the thousands of years of our existence. The interplay between these possibilities and realities makes helping our students learn a much more neurological and biological experience than many of us educators have ever thought.

Myths about the brain

We have several myths about the brain. And these myths are particularly out of date and damaging for teachers to hold. In the last few decades, scientists have been able to discover much more about the brain than we have ever known before. Here are some of the myths we as teachers need to discard[6].

- *The brain is a muscle.* The brain is not a muscle. Extended mental work does not always strengthen the brain. Learning does not increase from doing more homework exercises, for example.
- *We use only 10% of our brain.* Neuroscientists agree we all use close to 100% of our brain. The idea that our students are not using their brain is simply wrong.
- *Left brain and right brain thinking.* There is no left brain and right brain thinking in the sense that one person might be left brained, and another person might be able to develop right brained thinking. The left brain and right brain work together and communicate. There is as much difference within one hemisphere of the brain as between the two.

What we need to do as teachers is to learn more about the science of the brain, because understanding how the brain works has practical and significant implications for how we can teach better.

The brain is plastic

One day Julie Coates, also author of the pioneering book *Generational Learning Styles*, had her son come home from school and tell her that he had taken the Meyers Briggs learning style test and that he was and INTJ[7]. She thought that impossible, since she was an INTJ and she and her son learned completely differently. That initial experience led to her research on how generations learn differently, and to understanding a basic principle of the brain: the brain is plastic.

The brain changes over time. The brain can, and does, adjust to its environment. As the external environment changes, the brain can change to new conditions.

Thus, the brains of someone born in 1950 and someone born in 2000 are, in some significant ways, different.

Three areas of the brain

The cerebral cortex is a sheet of neural tissue that is outermost to the cerebrum of the brain. It covers the cerebrum and cerebellum, and is divided into left and right hemispheres. It has gray matter, and also white matter. There are 3 areas important to our understanding of how we learn in the cerebral cortex.

1. The rational brain. The rational brain, the neocortex or neopallium, is devoted to intellectual tasks. This is the area we as teachers most often associate with learning. Unfortunately, many teachers do not understand that the functioning of the rational brain does not stand alone, and is not necessarily independent of other areas of the brain. Instead, the rational brain is impacted by two other areas of the brain. The rational brain functions best only when these other two areas of the brain are at their ideal states.

2. The limbic system. The intermediate brain, the limbic system, or paleopallium, is devoted to emotions. The limbic system structures are involved in many of our emotions and motivations. Those feelings include anger, as well as pleasure. Certain structures of the limbic system are involved in memory as well.

Unfortunately, many teachers do not understand that the limbic system in a learner's brain has to be-in layperson's terms-settled or comfortable. If the limbic part of the brain is concerned with negative emotions, or dealing with emotional issues, then it is difficult for the rational part of the brain to engage in intellectual learning tasks. This is a major area where teachers need to focus, to help our learners be comfortable emotionally. When we as teachers demand, enforce, penalize, or demotivate, we diminish (not enhance) a student's mental ability to learn.

3. The primitive brain. The primitive brain, the archiopallium, is devoted to self preservation and aggression. When this part of the brain is activated, the person is practically unable to learn. The person's brain is virtually totally devoted to survival. Historically, that survival has been physical survival. But today, mental stress, verbal aggression, and other perceptions of attack in the modern world are just as real to a learner as a physical attack.

Unfortunately, many teachers do not understand that we as teachers are perceived by our learners as powerful authority figures, and as such we can do damage to our students careers, aspirations, feelings, and relationships. Teachers can and do put such stress on a learner that the student is functioning at the mental level of self-preservation. Whether intentional or not, we as teachers have to make doubly sure we are positive and encouraging with our learners.

It is often with the areas of the limbic system and primitive brain where outstanding teachers shine the most in enabling their students to learn.

The brain's emotional chemicals

Learning, it turns out, is both stimulated and rewarded by emotional chemicals in the brain. Professor James Zull[8] identifies three critical emotional brain chemicals that teachers should know about.

1. Adrenalin. You may know about adrenalin. It is a "fight or flight" emotional chemical. Stimulating adrenalin in your students, through unrealistic expectations, demands, negative comments, trying to "motivate your students," and other stress producing experiences, rarely produces positive learning results. Instead, it usually produces one or both of these reactions. A student will fight, defending him or herself, with body language, verbal comments, and sometimes behavior designed to protect. Or a student will engage in flight, emotionally shutting down, becoming more silent, and less engaged. Lesson: we as teachers should not engage in words or actions that produce stress in our students.

2. Dopamine. Dopamine is an emotional chemical produced as a reward. It is good. In fact, dopamine not only is a chemical produced as a result of learning, such as passing a test or winning a video game. It also serves to help connect neurons and adjust synapses in the brain, making them stronger, says Zull.

Zull says that the primary difference in a child's brain as it grows from 6 months old to 2 years old is not the presence of additional neurons in the brain, but the addition of more connections, or synapses, between those neurons. Learning, he thus implies, is about creating connections in the brain. "Emotions play a key role in changing connections," Zull notes.

When we learn, we mentally create movement, have a sense of having mentally moved from A to B, and dopamine is both a reward system and movement chemical. Lesson: we as teachers should seek to heighten reward and praise for our students learning, not diminish or fail to acknowledge learning. When we as teachers reward and praise, we support what dopamine does chemically to both reward learning and to stimulate further learning.

3. Serotonin. Serotonin is a mood chemical. It is involved with the regulation of mood, as well as some cognitive functions. When we as teachers create a safe online environment, that helps create a positive mood that then helps students learn.

Implications for teaching

In this section, we have seen how your teaching positively, or negatively, has a neurological outcome in the brain of each of your students. To summarize, much of our work in teaching is to help our students learn. Increasingly online, and to a growing extent in the face-to-face classroom, transferring information becomes less of a need as our students have access to an ever expanding universe of facts and data and information.

Instead, teaching today is more about a) making connections, helping our students to sort out and even dismiss much of the extraneous information and data, and help them focus on that information which is critical and important and is relevant to their learning; and b) providing an emotional atmosphere which creates a learning setting and then stimulates a student's learning and then rewards that student's progress and learning. The class environment is an environment where emotions are displayed, where you as an instructor can create emotions, and where you can help each student maximize his or her learning.

Motivation to Learn

The total of one's mental, emotional, physical and social states determines a person's motivation to learn. Much attention throughout history has been paid to how to motivate people. Generals have tried to motivate troops, supervisors have tried to motivate workers, salespeople have tried to motivate themselves, staffs have tried to motivate boards of directors, and boards of directors have tried to motivate staffs.

The quest for motivation has led to much thought on the subject as well. Those writing about the power of positive thinking can stay on the best seller list for weeks or even years, and those speaking about it can fill halls with rallies on motivation.

Most authorities on adult learning advocate self-directed learning. For example, author Laurent Daloz says, "We teachers sometimes speak of pushing our students to higher stages of development. We want the best for them after all, and need to know that we have made a difference in their lives - an important difference. To push a person to change is about as effective in the long run as trying to push a chain uphill. People develop best under their own power."[9] As a teacher, you will doubtless be confronted by people with a range of motivations. How much time you want to spend stimulating motivation is up to you.

This author's experience is that almost all people want to learn. A given person may not want to learn a specific subject in a specific way at a specific time, but that person is nevertheless motivated to learn provided there is a subject of interest engaged with his or her own learning style.

Most adult learning experts agree that while motivation comes from the learner, responsibility for motivation to learn rests not only with the learner, but also with the teacher and program administration.

You as a teacher can help or hinder another person's attempts to learn. By failing to recognize limits, by ignoring or even constructing barriers, by not understanding how a person learns, you can be a negative influence on someone's learning. By facilitating learning and helping your participants, you can be a positive influence.

Chapter 3.
Helping Adults Learn

"Those having torches will pass them on to others."

— Plato, famous ancient Greek philosopher

Gilford Highet in *The Art of Teaching* retells the story of the famous orchestra conductor Toscanini, who once arrived on tour in a new city and took over an orchestra he had never conducted before. He started conducting and after a minute or two noticed that the first violin player looked off. He was playing well enough, but his face was all distorted, and when he turned a page of the score, he grimaced as though he were in great pain.

Toscanini stopped the orchestra and said, "Concert-master! Are you ill?" The first violin's face at once returned to normal. "No, thank you," he said, "I'm quite all right, maestro. Please go on."

"Very well, if you're sure you're fit," Toscanini said. "Begin at D, please, gentlemen." And off they went again. But the next time Toscanini glanced at the first violin, he saw him looking worse than ever. His face was all drawn up to one side, his teeth were showing between wolfish lips, and his brow was furrowed with deep clefts. He was sweating painfully and breathing hard.

"One moment please. Concert-master, you really look ill. Do you want to go home?"

"No, no, no, Mr. Toscanini. Please go ahead."

"But I insist," said Toscanini. "What's wrong? Are you having an attack? Would you like to lie down for a while?"

"No, I'm not ill," said the first violin.

"Well what on earth is the matter?" asked Toscanini. "You look awful, you have been making the most agonizing faces, and you're obviously suffering ...."

"To be quite frank," said the first violin, "I hate music."

To teach well, one must enjoy it. As the educator Kenneth Eble says, "I hold to one of the oldest views of nature, that learning is fun."[1] And if learning is to be fun, teaching must be enjoyable as well.

As we saw in the previous chapter, adults are self-motivated, interested, and usually eager to participate. Teaching adults, then, is not so much trying to convince, cajole, or tutor, as it is helping adults learn.

In fact, recently, people have been trying to coin a term other than "teacher" to describe the person who helps adults learn, including "trainer," "facilitator," "manager of the learning environment," "resource person," "group leader," and "convener." Until another term replaces it, we shall stay with the word "teacher," but do so recognizing that the teacher of adults needs a different set of attributes, skills, and understandings than other teachers do.

The teacher of adults must have empathy, interest, and a feel for people and teaching as much as the expertise in the subject being covered. Knowing what not to do is as important as what to do in teaching adults.

People are not necessarily born with good teaching traits. The great orator may be born, the genius may be born, but adults can learn to teach other adults. There are good teachers, of course, and poor ones, but all teachers can improve.

Attributes of a Good Teacher

We can describe the most commonly accepted characteristics of what makes a teacher of adults effective. But the descriptions will be general, and denote attitudes and basic skills. It may even leave you a bit unsatisfied; and that is simply because there is no *one way* to teach adults.

Nevertheless, it helps to talk about the kind of teacher people respond to most of the time. Even if you cannot develop every skill to the fullest, if you are sincere about becoming a good teacher, you probably will succeed. One of the chief characteristics of adult learners is that they appreciate and sympathize with someone who is trying.

Educator Frank C. Pearce describes the ideal teacher of adults as "people-centered, more interested in people than things, more interested in individuality than conformity, more interested in finding solutions than in following rules. The teacher must have understanding, flexibility, patience, humor, practicality, creativity and preparation."

One must meet three requirements before being able to teach adults:

- a basic competence in the subject,
- a desire to share one's knowledge,
- a wish to help adults learn.[2]

Basic competence. The first requirement has intimidated many potentially good teachers of adults because they have mistaken a basic competence for exceptional competence. Although the more one knows about a subject, the more one can share, most people underrate their competence rather than overrate it. If you have a basic competence and are honest about your skills and experience in describing the course, by all means teach.

Desire to share one's knowledge. The second requirement is essential. Someone with a basic subject competence will likely be a far better teacher with a desire to share it, than would be a subject expert without a desire to share it.

A wish to help adults learn. The third requirement is not only critical, but becoming more important than simply a subject expertise. Helping adults learn is such an essential teaching skill that it should occupy more of your time and attention than the subject material.

In evaluating classes, the problem most students point to least is the teacher's knowledge of the subject. Most student complaints are not about the teacher's knowledge of the subject but the teacher's ability to share that knowledge.

Furthermore, teachers of adults acquire much of their competence by doing and experience. Credentials play a minor part in the teacher's credibility and the student's interest in one's teaching ability. The old saying, "He who can, does; he who cannot, teaches," just doesn't hold true for teaching adults. In most adult learning, it is the person who can who does the teaching.

Skills You Should Have

Some general skills or talents apply to any teaching situation. Here are a few basic skills you should have or develop for the best possible teaching experience.

Listening. Listening is as important as effective speaking. And it is important to effective teaching because much learning takes place when a participant is expressing an idea. The attention a student receives when speaking can encourage his or her learning interest, or inhibit it. A teacher can listen and encourage the student speaking by some sort of acknowledgement, either a verbal "uh huh" or "I see," or nonverbal cues, such as a nod or smile. And a teacher can stimulate more discussion with what are called "door openers," such as "Would you like to talk about it?" or "Would you like to say more?"

Listening tips. Educator Steven Brookfield suggests that you also should encourage active listening among other participants. "A good part of discussion participation is directed to listening carefully to others' ideas... for people who are used to talking, not listening and having their voice heard rather than hearing others, this kind of active listening is one of the most valuable intellectual activities they can experience."[3]

Professor Russell Robinson, in *Helping Adults Learn and Change,* says the listener should:

- try to understand what is meant, not get ready to reply, contradict or refute,
- not interpret too quickly what the speaker is saying,
- put aside his own views,
- not jump ahead of the speaker,
- not prepare his answer while listening,
- be interested and alert and show it,
- not interrupt,
- expect the speaker's language to be different from his own,
- provide feedback,
- avoid negative feedback.[4]

Helping insecure learners. Learners who lack confidence in themselves are common in adult learning. A good teacher needs to make the learning environment secure for these people. Building their confidence is not condescending, but keeps their desire to learn alive.

In adult learning, enhancing security promotes learning. One of the ways to encourage the unconfident learner is through reward. That reward can be verbal reinforcement. Or it can be a smile, nod, or even occasionally a physical expression, such as a handshake, pat on the back, touch on the arm, or a hug.

Australian Philip C. Candy, in his book *Self Direction for Lifelong Learning,* has this to say about enhancing security: "Educators who hold high expectations for their students tend to convey these through complex and subtle patterns of interaction, which commonly result in the learners living up to these expectations, and in the process, developing a more positive image of themselves."[5] Sometimes learners will demean themselves, professing inadequacy, frustration, or outside interference.

Tips for helping frustrated learners. When the learner is unhappy about some situation, focus on how the student feels about the external situation, and do not focus on the student's own feelings of frustration. When someone begins demeaning themselves, you should do the following:

- don't contradict the person's views;
- don't use logical explanations;
- don't ridicule that person's views;
- do convey your positive regard for the person.[6]

Wrong things. One of the skills a teacher needs to develop is handling situations in which the learner is doing something wrong. Here are some wrong situations and how to correct them.

- When the other person is doing the wrong thing,
  - don't talk to the person, but to the condition;
  - describe what you see;
  - describe what you feel;
  - describe what needs to be done;
  - say nothing to the person about himself or herself.[7]
- Some students prefer to be quiet and learn that way. Privacy deserves respect, but there are some overtures you as the teacher can make without intruding. Patience, invitations to speak, and other strategies, like dividing into subgroups or games, may involve quiet learners without embarrassing them.

- "You" messages are bad, especially when things are not going right. Robinson says to avoid saying things like "You must," "You should," "You do it now," "You always," "You never," or "You act like..." Instead, "I" messages are less offensive, and help turn the situation around. Say, "I'm frustrated by this noise," or "I'm really annoyed when people interrupt me."[8]

- When the adult learner does something wrong, don't punish that person, verbally or nonverbally. Adult educators are unanimous in their disapproval of punishment and negative reinforcement. It is counterproductive to learning. Punishment has inhibited more learning in a person's lifetime, and indeed throughout history, than any other single factor.

We can't say it strongly enough. Don't punish.

Supportive actions. Certain words, phrases, gestures, or actions will go far in building a supportive atmosphere in which your participants will feel able to grow, learn, and respond to the group and your leadership. Try:

- a smile;
- responding to a raised hand;
- a pat on the shoulder;
- an expression of enthusiasm;
- genuine pleasure at seeing your participants again;
- listening with patience;
- warm attentiveness to others;
- helping a student with difficulty.

It may seem repetitive, but adult students learn best when they feel secure, and supportive words will build that security.

Humor. Although few of us are stand-up comics, many situations in the class will prompt a laugh or a smile. Take advantage of them, and use them well. Humor is good therapy. It puts people at ease, allows them to relax a little, and helps tensions disappear. Humor helps promote learning.

Here are some tips on using humor effectively.

- Don't be afraid to use a joke if it is appropriate and is not overdone. Even a poor joke will be recognized as a good try.

24

- Allow and encourage a little laughter and good fun. Don't stifle it unless it gets out of hand. There are usually pleasant and humorous situations in the class, and the teacher can take the lead in laughing a little at them.
- Laugh at yourself. Laughing at others is hardly positive, but you can afford to point to one of your mistakes and invite the others to enjoy it.
- If someone else in the class has the gift of humor, you can play off it or invite a comment or two from time to time.
- If you don't have the knack for humor, don't try to force it. Smile a lot, be cheerful and pleasant, and just as much good will can flow from that.

Steps in Positive Teaching

From the beginning of your class through the end, you want to build and then maintain what is called a positive learning climate, an atmosphere in which your students feel comfortable, are both part of the group and maintain their own individuality, respect and enjoy your leadership and the talents of the other members of the class, and are able to learn through positive reinforcement and caring.

There is not one correct way to build that climate; each teacher must do it his or her own way. If you are yourself, being honest, positive, interested in others, and friendly, you can set the tone. By carefully bringing in each member of the group, trying to recognize each participant in some way, you can create a good group. By welcoming dissent or disagreement and individual expression, you can enhance individuality. By reward and positive reinforcement rather than emphasis on error and mistake, you can promote learning and the stimulus to learn. In these ways, a positive climate is built, one in which you can teach, and they can learn.

You cannot be too positive and encouraging. If being super-positive is difficult for you, remember teaching is not about you, it's about your learners. And being positive, enthusiastic and encouraging does increase their learning.

In *Yes, You Can Teach*, Florence Nelson outlines the four steps of encouragement to maintain the learning climate throughout the class. Encouragement is not always effusive praise. Providing encouragement can be a subtle art, and it is a changing process depending on the needs of the learner. Nelson

25

points to a four-step process that helps the learner become self-directed while lessening the role of the teacher. It illustrates that the best teachers are those who can step aside when the learner is ready.

These are the four steps of encouragement:

1. **The fundamentals.** In the beginning, effusive praise like "great," "wonderful," and "keep going."

2. **Pleasing you the teacher.** As they advance, let them know, "It is coming along well," "Now that you've got the right idea," and so on.

3. **Pleasing you and themselves.** Still further along, with comments like, "Yes, that's it. .. how do you feel about it?" or "I can see some progress here. What do you think?" or "I'll bet you're proud of yourself."

4. **Pleasing themselves.** And finally, when the learner is well along, you can step aside and say, "When you need help, just let me know."[9]

Chapter 4.
Tackling Learning Styles

"Mrs. Gascoyne said they didn't want to treat me differently from everyone else in the school because then everyone would want to be treated differently and it would set a precedent."

— Christopher in *The Curious Incident of the Dog in the Night-Time*

Adults participating in a course have always been complicated, with individual characteristics and learning styles. Yet one of the primary aims of the last century was to develop conformity in skills and knowledge. Thus the typical class has resembled a factory setting in many ways, with the participants all expected to be at the same point and have the same level of accomplishment.

Teachers have often followed the factory model by teaching only one way. Once I overheard this conversation between a teacher and a learner who was behind in math:

Teacher: "I could teach you math a different way."

Learner: "Why don't you?"

Teacher: "Because I'm the teacher."

This is the wrong approach. Yet slowly but surely, teaching is moving from the delivery of content to helping adults learn. One reason is that, in the 21st century, the workplace is increasingly valuing individual strengths rather than conformity in skills. Another reason is simply that we know more now about learning styles, and that we do not all learn in the same way.

There is a fascinating growth of research about the brain and how our physical, neurological and hormonal make-up affects how we each learn. This learning research regarding nature has been accompanied by learning research regarding nurture. As a result, others have been studying how social and cultural forces affect how we each learn. Together, the research is helping us as teachers understand and address our participants' different learning styles.

There are several different ways of looking at learning styles. Some of them include:

- Sensory learning styles
- Gender learning styles
- Generational learning styles
- Ethnic and cultural learning styles
- Neurological learning styles.

Vary your teaching. In terms of your teaching, the implications of learning styles is that you should vary your teaching with different techniques to respond to different kinds of learning styles, advises the great adult educator Jerry Apps. Do not teach to one learning style. Even learners with a predominant learning style will benefit from a variety of teaching and learning techniques. So the lesson is not to teach to a learner's style, but to vary your techniques and to include various teaching styles.

Sensory Learning Styles

The traditional way we have understood learning styles is that many of us have a preference in how we use our senses to learn. There are:

- **Visual learners,** who prefer to see or read something.
- **Auditory learners,** who may retain more knowledge by listening.
- **Motion (kinesthetic) learners,** who need to touch, practice or actually perform the function or task in order to learn it. For example, if you are talking about a novel, an auditory learner may retain more by listening to the book on tape. And if you are discussing how to organize a home office, a touch learner may understand it better by actually moving furniture around.

Gender Learning Styles

Men and women learn differently. And because males and females mature at different rates, there are even greater distinctions between how boys and girls learn.[1]

Men are generally better at learning spatial relationships (for example, maps and directions), math, science and technology skills. Women are generally better at verbal skills, language, and written communication.

Women mostly enjoy relationships and like group learning, while more men prefer learning independently. Women find it far easier than most men to express feelings, and are able to communicate feelings more quickly than men are.

Men generally have a harder time hearing than most women. In a one-to-one situation, most men prefer the teacher to sit next to them or side-by-side. Generally women prefer someone to sit across from or directly facing them.

Males are far more likely to doodle, fiddle, and stare out the window than women. Males have a shorter attention span, and benefit from more frequent exercise or physical activity.

Females are likely to be able to sit longer and smile far more often than males. In school and college, girls turn their homework in on time. Males are more likely to disagree with or argue with an instructor. In school and college, boys often turn their home work in late.

On a bell curve with the average learner in the middle of the curve, there are apt to be more males at the low end (lower performing) of the curve. Also there are apt to be more males at the upper end (higher performing) of the curve. Women are more likely to be clustered closer to the median or average.[2]

All of these gender learning styles originate in the neurology and hormonal differences between males and females. For example, males do not want to fidget. Instead, males have less serotonin than females and use fidgeting as a way to focus. Males do not want to be devoid of expressing their feelings. Instead, the synapses between the neurons associated with feeling and the neurons associated with verbal expression are not as well connected as they are for females.

It is critical for us as teachers not to attach motivation or "want to" labels to learning phenomenon that are clearly neurological and hormonal in origin.

Generational Learning Styles

We now have four different generations engaged in lifelong learning. Julie Coates has written the definitive work called *Generational Learning Styles*. Her work is summarized here.

- Seniors are those adults born in or before 1945.
- Baby Boomers are those adults born between 1946 and 1964.
- Gen Xers were born between 1965 and 1979.
- Gen Y learners were born between 1980 and 2000.

Coates has shown that learning interests and styles do not just vary by age, they also differ by generation.[3] She offers these tips.

Tips for teaching Seniors

- Be polite. Say "please" and "thank you."
- Use proper grammar-all the time. Otherwise, your credibility is shot.
- Don't use off-color language or humor. It's a major turn-off to seniors.
- Older learners, especially, like to interact with people, not machines.
- If you're using computers in your instruction, provide plenty of opportunity for personal interaction.
- Make sure all visual materials are clear and easy to read, with print that is large enough to see easily.
- Do provide a summary of the class topics and goals. Clarity is essential for understanding direction with this group.
- Be pleasant but not "personal." Sharing personal stories or anecdotes can be a great way to illustrate a point or to communicate an idea, but don't get too intimate.
- Don't put them on the spot or do anything that could be embarrassing to the learner. Let them volunteer their comments. Don't call on them without giving them some preparation time.

Tips for teaching Baby Boomers

- Be democratic. Treat them as "equals."
- Respect their experience. Acknowledge what they know.
- Treat them as though they're young, even if they're not. Ask lots of

questions and acknowledge what they know.

- Just because you're in charge, don't think they accept that you're the authority. Dialogue and participation is key for this group. Don't be authoritarian. Boomers have authority problems, and they'll turn off quickly if they think you're bossing them around. Boomers are text oriented and like to read. Boomers feel they should read everything assigned, and find it difficult to scan or be selective in what to read.

- Boomers are not oriented to multimedia and even regard multimedia as frivolous or entertainment rather than a learning tool. Boomers feel a course can solve just about any problem, are attracted to the experience or journey of learning, and like the word "learning."

Tips for teaching Gen Xers

- Gen Xers like a fun, informal environment.

- They are outcomes or results oriented. They do not entertain learning for learning's sake.

- Authoritarianism is ineffective or counterproductive.

- Clear statements of expectations and consistency are necessary. Gen Xers are highly visual and appreciate design and color. Gen Xers are easily bored and require content to be relevant. This generation seems "unmotivated," or "without" a work ethic to many Baby Boomers. The "slacker" image is really an attitude or value that balances work with family, friendships and leisure.

- Gen Xers do not want to waste time.

- Gen Xers are more technically oriented than older generations. When technology achieves a result faster than a meeting, they choose communicating via technology.

Tips for teaching Gen Yers

- Gen Yers have a stricter moral code and care about manners. They want more supervision and structure.

- Gen Yers like more attention from authority figures.

- Lively and varied teaching and learning techniques work best. They are very into the Internet and web, immersed in technology. Many cannot read or write cursive and find handwriting useless. Visually similar to Xers - multiple focal points and they like multimedia.

- Gen Y learners are readers, so provide more back-up info. They like lots of feedback and affirmation.
- Give them lots of structure for expectations.
- Gen Yers learn collaboratively (in groups) and from each other.

For more on how different generations learn, see *Generational Learning Styles* by Julie Coates, available from LERN.

Ethnic and Cultural Learning Styles

People from different ethnic groups and cultures may have some distinct learning styles specific to their cultural heritage. Some examples:

- **Personal distance.** In some cultures, people stand closer or farther away from another person than what you might be used to.
- **Discussion involvement.** In some cultures, speaking to a teacher is a sign of challenge to authority. Engaging learners from such cultures in discussion may be a challenge.
- **Signs of respect differ.** For example, my foster son came from a particular African American culture where, for historical reasons, looking at someone in the eyes was a sign of disrespect. His teachers did not understand that when he looked away from them, it was a sign of respect, not the reverse.

As a teacher, you can do at least two things to help understand your learners from other cultures. First, you can read or ask someone about learning differences from a particular culture.

Second, and most importantly, when you encounter a behavior that you do not understand or perceive as being negative, simply suspend any judgment and ask someone about the possibility of a cultural difference.

Neurological Learning Styles

Neurological learning styles are those that are hard-wired and a consequence of neurological differences among us. We are moving away from seeing these differences as "disabilities." We are starting to understand that no one is "normal" and that everyone has some neurological differences from others. For us as teachers, the goal is no longer to perceive and treat people as normal and abnormal. The goal now is to tap into each person's strengths and help each learner overcome or adapt to his or her weaknesses.

As you can see, each learner has a complicated set of learning styles, preferences and abilities. And we have not even discussed other learning style and personality tests, which abound. The tendency for us as teachers might be to give up and just teach one way, addressing a non-existent "average learner."

Instead, I encourage taking one small step at a time. Tackle the issue of learning styles as it relates to your participants. See this as an exciting opportunity rather than an overwhelming impossibility.

The most important mistake to avoid is mistaking a learner's style as a lack of motivation. This is one of the most common teacher cop-outs or excuses.

Everyone is motivated to learn, given the proper circumstances. With just one comment or action, you can make a big difference in helping someone with a particular learning style. Here are some tips.

- **Listen.** The more we listen to a learner, the more likely we are to find the teaching answers.

- **Ask.** We do not ask our learners often enough about what concerns or troubles us.

- **Provide choices.** Since learning styles differ, providing only one way or the same way for everyone may not be fair or equal. One of the greatest tools we as teachers have is to provide our learners with choices.

- **Use the web.** The Internet can address learners as individuals. On the web, learning can be customized and individualized. *Use other learners.* Consider using buddies, peer teaching, mentoring, and other ways of involving fellow participants in learning from each other.

Part II.
Developing Your Course

Chapter 5.
How Knowledge is Now Organized

Knowledge is actually organized differently now because of the invention of the Internet. This new structuring of knowledge changes the way we as teachers construct content for our courses.

Five new principles of how knowledge is organized are:

1. Course content can be unlimited.
2. Course content goes deeper, not down.
3. Course content is best organized by units.
4. Course content can be posted online and become permanent and reusable.
5. Course content and resources online can be shared.

What this means for you the teacher is that you and I now have to organize the content and information of our courses differently. It also means we have the advantages and benefits of online resources, both your own work and the work of many others, available to enhance your participants' learning.

Course content is now unlimited

The tremendous growth of knowledge and information now means that essentially information for any subject area is now unlimited. Today there is more information and knowledge than any one person, any group, any society, any organization could possibly acquire. And new knowledge and information is being created at a faster rate than ever before.

Adults born before 1965 grew up in a time when the amount of knowledge was more manageable, when one could start at the beginning and read to the end. So people growing up in the 20th century read left to right, top to bottom, start to finish. This is not how young people on the Internet read. Because there is too much information, reading on the Internet becomes a process of discovery.

A second and related force affecting how knowledge is organized is the growing specialization and segmentation of knowledge and information.

New jobs are being created every day. New disciplines, subdisciplines, and areas of study are being created every day.

To cope, people in the workforce concentrate or focus on increasingly smaller areas of knowledge, or specialties. And people are segmented into narrower and narrower interest groups.

This increasing specialization means that one can take a course and divide it up into ten different parts and offer a whole course on each of the ten different parts. And then one can take each of the ten different parts, divide them again into subparts and offer a whole course on each of the one hundred subparts.

Focus your course content on what is critical to know. What this means for you the teacher is that your job is now to focus your course content on what is critical and important. There's lots of 'nice' information out there. But your learners have limited time. They want you to tell them what is important, and what is not as important.

Course content goes deeper, not down

Before the Internet, information was organized like a book. There was a beginning, middle and end. And one was expected to read and know all of the information. But with information now unlimited, we have to think not about going down the page, but going deeper. Web sites are organized to go deeper. Information on a web site is organized like a complicated set of ladders, where you start at the top and go "deeper," choosing which ladder you want to use next. It is the very same method that students used to use to outline a report. The outline went like this:

I. xxxx
II. xxxx
  A. xxxx
  B. xxxxx
    1. xxxx
    2. xxxx
      a) xxxx
      b) xxxx, etc.

All items with the same type of designation (I, II, III, etc., A, B, C, etc.) have roughly equivalent importance and are distinct from each other. When items appear indented within a larger category (for example, B., followed by 1.2.) that means the items are within the same general category and are subtopics or specialized information.

This is how web sites are organized. My master web developer, Cem Erdem, designed a web site schema for me this way:

Home Page

I	II	III
A. B.		A. B. C.
1. 2.		1. 2. 3.
a) b) c)		etc.

IA.2.c) would probably be something more in-depth and specific in the whole area of whatever information I,A is about. A screen of copy for IA.2.c) would be "deeper" than I or IIIB., for example. IA. and IB. would be more closely related in subject matter than IB. and IIIB., for instance.

Organize advanced course content to go deeper. What this means for you the teacher is that you can and should provide more advanced, detailed or specific information and content. But structure advanced or specific content like a web site, with information going deeper, giving your learners choice, ladders and paths.

Course Content is best organized by units

Course content is now best organized by "units." Susan Kirshbaum, head of online learning products for Oracle, a large software company involved with storing data and information, says that a course used to be thought of as

39

a single identity, a huge "glob" as she calls it.[1]

Adds Guenther Weydauer, Vice President for New Product Development at LearningByte International, a content development company, "the worst kind of course content architecture is a bunch of HTML documents thrown together."[2]

Course design has changed.

Knowledge is now being broken apart and broken down. The once-whole glob course is now composed of units, sometimes called or thought of as modules or lessons. Each unit is a separate entity, with a separate focus or theme or set of concepts or skills. Taken together the units make up a course. Broken down, each unit is itself an interesting, almost-independent entity.

Units can be broken down further into subunits. A subunit might be a page of copy, on which there is a single central thought or idea. Subunits are arranged in a way that makes sense and compose a unit. But subunits might be broken apart and each might be used again in a different course.

Here's how it breaks down:

- Curriculum (a set of related courses that compose the entire study)
- Course (a complete course of study, with a beginning and an end)
- Units (usually from 5 to 15 independent and different lessons, each with a different focus or theme)
- Subunits (a smaller breakdown of knowledge with a single focus or concept)

Design your course with units. What this means for teachers is that we all should now structure and design our courses using units. A unit may also be a week or class meeting, or a chapter in a book. But that's not how you should think about it and plan. Think about and plan your units as each being a distinct concept, technique, idea or theme. A unit has three aspects to it:

1. Content
2. Interaction
3. Assessment

So for each unit, you will of course have content. But you will also want to have discussion or some other kind of interaction with your learners around the content of the unit. And you will want to have some kind of assessment, such as a quiz, also based on the content of the unit.

Course content can be posted online and become permanent and reusable

You most likely will have hard copy content and resources, such as a book or handouts. And that's great. Hard copy resources do aid in learning and not all hard copy resources should be replaced by online resources. But now you can also post content online for your learners. While you may make some modifications, essentially you only have to do this once and it becomes permanent and can be reused for your course in the future.[3]

What the research shows is that learners in courses that incorporate online learning in some fashion, often called "hybrid" courses, learn more than people who only have traditional classroom meetings and resources. As an aside, the research also shows that learners in hybrid courses learn more than learners in purely online courses.

Incorporate online resources in your course. What this means for you the teacher is that your participants will learn more, and have a better experience, if you incorporate some online resources in your course and make them available to your participants.

Course content and resources online can be shared

You can supplement your course content with other online resources. While you the teacher may create content for your course, there are now numerous sources of online content available to supplement and enhance your course content.

Instead of creating, rewriting, and reinventing pieces of data or knowledge, researchers, authors, professors and others (including maybe you) have created subunits of knowledge or information.

Then anytime someone wants to use that subunit of information in a course, the information is available and can be used, following copyright and fair use guidelines for educational material. Much content can be used for free. Several benefits then accrue.

• The best information and knowledge is available and widely used.

• It doesn't have to be recreated time and time again.

• It is presented in its best form, illustrated and conveyed in the best

41

possible manner for maximum understanding and learning.

The reusable units of data are organized into learning objects. Another name is "shareable content objects," or SCOs. A learning object or shareable content object is content that is reusable and shareable, that is, can be used at different times in different courses sponsored by various institutions or providers. According to Weydauer, a SCO:

- is 10-20 minutes of learning (in written, audio, video or other form).
- has 5-15 learning interactions taking place within it.
- satisfies a small number of learning objectives.
- has an inter-operability connector which allows others to access the SCO.

Utilize some of the many online resources available. What this means for you the teacher is that you can, and should, utilize some of the many online resources available in your course. There are videos, audio presentations, slides, pictures, charts, readings, web sites and many other resources. Choose those that complement and enhance your course content and respond to different learning styles.

This is a fundamentally new way of approaching the development of a course, and it offers exciting possibilities for enhancing quality and serving your learners better.

Chapter 6.
Preparing the Course

"It's a very tricky business, teaching"

— Gilford Highet, author of *The Art of Teaching*

Every course needs preparation. Without it, your thoughts will be disjointed, the course structure fragmented, and the students will feel as though... well, you hadn't prepared. The dangers of under preparation are many. You can forget points. You can give details out of sequence and confuse your students. You can talk too long and not leave time for other important topics. You can forget a visual aid or handout that would have helped in your presentation.

Teaching is not just talking. Even though you may know the subject thoroughly, a lack of preparation will make you look as if you don't know what you are talking about. Teachers have thought they could go into a situation and just start talking. Ideas would flow spontaneously because they know the subject so well. It just doesn't happen that way. Just as all those ad lib jokes you hear comedians "spontaneously" come up with are on index cards some where in a joke file, your remarks should be planned as well for maximum effect. Other teachers have thought they would sit down and say, "Well, what do you want to talk about?" and let the students ask questions to get the ball rolling. But students rarely can start asking questions about a topic they have not thought about before, and the chances of this latter tactic working are slim.

Every course takes preparation. If you taught the course before, it might take less preparation, but you still need to think about your next class as unique. If you have taught the course several times, you may need to prepare to make it different from others to avoid becoming stale and conveying the "yellowed lecture notes" feeling students have when they think the teacher has repeated it too often.

Goals, Objectives, and End Results

Before looking at each meeting separately, take a broad look at the course as a whole. What are the goals, objectives, and end results of the class?[1]

Goals. Goals are long-term wishes. They are the reason you are teaching but are not necessarily achievable by the end of the course. The goal of a class on twentieth century art may be a greater appreciation of art, and the goal for a class on investing wisely may be to help make the students financially independent. But neither goal is likely to be accomplished in the short time you are meeting. Look at your goals for the class. What do you want to happen in the class? Are the class goals consistent with your reasons for teaching this course in the first place? If they are not, you need to revise the course. If you are not satisfied with the course goals, your students will feel the negative effect.

Second, what would be a learner's goal in taking the class? Your students are time conscious and problem oriented, and perhaps their goals for the class may differ from yours. Their goals may not be an appreciation for art, but enough knowledge to get through the Louvre on their next trip to Paris. Their goals might not be financial independence, but doubling their current savings accounts. Teacher and learner goals are not incompatible, and you need to think about their goals and perspectives when you plan the course. By achieving the learner's goals you might just achieve yours as well.

The ideal way to meet your learners' goals is to sit down with them before the class starts and invite them to help plan the course with you. As you learn their goals for the class, you can then go back and prepare the course with their specific needs and interests in mind. If you ever have the opportunity to plan your course with the students, take advantage of this experience. Unfortunately, most classes need to begin when the students first come together, and the course must be planned in advance. For most groups, you have to plan ahead with the students in mind, and then revise the course next time when you learn more about the students' needs.

Some preparing and revising can be done with the students, mostly on the modification level rather than on overall goals and the broader outline. The teacher should seek the students' help in the first session or even others, and then try to adjust somewhat to meet those particular interests and needs. By taking even five minutes to address a student's question, you can make the whole course positive and fulfilling for that student and show the others your willingness to meet their agenda, not just your own.

Objectives. Objectives differ from goals because they are quantified and time delineated. Although to appreciate art is a goal, to be able to identify Van Gogh from Monet in three weeks is an objective. For some classes, like a discussion of women's literature, goals may be much more important and evident than objectives. But for many other classes, from dance to job-related skills, objectives are important to adult students who want to acquire a specific knowledge and for whom the success of the class may depend on their ability to learn something they can use immediately.

End results. Along with objectives for the course, you need to think of the end results. Where do you want your students to be at the end of the course compared with where they were at the beginning?

Before you start to think about the content of the course, you should have three things clearly in mind and down on paper:

The course: A. Goals, B. Objectives, C. End results.

Sample Course: Planting Strawberries

Goals:

1. To convey an appreciation for the taste of natural, homegrown fresh strawberries;

2. To encourage local residents to plant more strawberries;

3. To start a Strawberry Club for home growers interested in sharing knowledge and selling extra strawberries.

Objectives:

1. To compare the taste of homegrown natural strawberries with store bought strawberries;

2. To demonstrate how to plant strawberries, including when, where, and how;

3. To show how to care for and pick strawberries;

4. To have each participant help in planting a number of strawberry plants.

End Results:

1. Students will know the difference in taste between store bought and homegrown strawberries;
2. Students will know how to plant strawberries at home.

Amount of Material

Having defined your goals, objectives, and end results, you then can estimate how much material to cover in the course. This is not always easy. Sometimes a class may get caught up in discussion and cover only a small fraction of what you have intended; other times, the participants catch on sooner than you anticipated and you are racing through the material. As a teacher, you should be prepared for both outcomes, having enough material available and yet being able to trim and cut back to the most essential points if the discussions or explanations take longer than planned. A long discussion on a particular point is a more positive sign of involvement and learning than is a silent audience. Covering many ideas may not be a sign of faster learning. Questions, discussions, and disagreement over one single idea may mean more learning than quiet acceptance of a whole series of points.

There are various ways to arrange your material, and different means to gauge how much to put in any one course. One way is to divide the material into three categories: material essential for the students to know; material important for the students to know; and material that is nice for the students to know. Then you can make sure you convey what is essential, try to work in as much important material as possible, and add what is nice to know if you have time. With time running short, cut out the nice-to-know material and then the important items, and concentrate only on the essential points.

Slant or Approach

The goals for the class, particularly those of the learners, will determine the slant or approach you take with your subject. Every subject can be approached from many different directions and provide different end results and competencies. And the slant or approach may determine the success of the class. You could do a historical approach to car mechanics, or help people fix their own cars. You could talk about Italian cooking in general, or zero in on sauces as a subtopic. You could talk about modern novels, or relate them to the problems of interpersonal relationships and the change in family structure today. Here are eight ways you can slant the course.

1. **Basics.** A simple introductory course for people with little or no knowledge about the subject.

2. **Advanced.** New items people with a basic knowledge are unlikely to know.

3. **Subtopics.** Taking one particular area within the subject matter and concentrating or specializing on this.

4. **Demonstration.** Showing the class members how something is done or how something works.

5. **Practical, how-to.** Emphasizing the mechanics of the topic.

6. **They do it.** The participants actually learn by doing and come away with an ability they didn't have before.

7. **Current.** Focusing on the latest changes or trends in the subject area.

8. **Relating.** How the topic relates to some other topic, current event, or problem.

A course on bicycles could be slanted any number of ways. For example:

• an introduction to the workings of a bike (basic);

• a look at wind flow, BTUs and human energy in bike speed (advanced);

• cable brakes on a 10-speed bike (subtopic);

• see how bikes are made, a trip through a bike factory (demonstration);

• repairing your bike (they do it, how-to); vectors and the bike of the future (current); bicycles and urban pollution (relating).

By taking the wrong slant, a course can miss the mark and not meet participant expectations. On the other hand, an unsuccessful course can be turned into a successful one by taking a different slant. With so many different approaches to any given topic, one subject can be turned into many different courses, each one appealing to a different kind of learner.

After determining the slant and the amount of material you can cover in one course, the content can be organized to deliver it in the best way possible. Here are four ways in which content can be organized for delivery.

1. **Simple to complex.** Start with the easily understood, move to the harder.

2. **General to specific.** Start with an overall scheme or theme, and then get down to the specific items within that overall picture.

3. **Concrete to abstract.** Start with the here and now before moving to theories or concepts.

4. **Chronological sequence.** A historical sequence, starting at the beginning and working through history to today. Or another time sequence.[1]

With your goals, objectives, end results, and material organized, you then can break the course down into each session or meeting.

Typical divisions for an individual class meeting include:

• Introduction
• Why the topic to be discussed is important
• The central theme or concept
• Elaborations on the theme or main point
• Examples or demonstrations
• Applications, conclusions or results
• Summary of the main points
• Questions and answers
• A look ahead to the next class.

Tim Wentling, in his book *Planning for Effective Training,* out- lines the following steps in preparing an individual session:

• Identify the knowledge necessary to accomplish the objective.
• Identify the performance/skill requirements of each objective.
• Identify important attitude elements for the objective. Organize the knowledge, skill and attitude elements into a logical sequence.
• Record the topical outline on the lesson plan.[2]

Educator Russ Robinson, in *Helping Adults Learn and Change,* advocates coming up with a title for each session or meeting. Selecting a title for

48

every meeting also illustrates a key point: that each class meeting is a separate entity.

Each class session is like a short story. It should have a beginning and an end. And the student should take something away from every class. When each session is a neat unit, the student will remember more easily what is covered, tend not to confuse issues or topics, and be able to do or know something at the end of each class. The participant can then justify to himself or herself and to others why to return next time.

To do this, make up a worksheet for each class session. It does not have to be elaborate, nor long, but it will help you plan the session. Here is a simple outline for a class session, organized for delivery.

CLASS	SESSION NUMBER OR TITLE		
Objective	Content Outline	Techniques	Time

In each class session, you will be selling the whole course again because, if the participant doesn't learn from each class, he or she may not be interested enough to return.

Unlike the school situation in which the students have to attend, you cannot afford to ramble too much, be too disorganized, or bore the participants. A little simple planning can help you avoid those mistakes.

After you have outlined the course goals and content, you can move from what you will say to ways you will say it. It is important to keep in mind four points in planning teaching techniques for your course.

1. **Keep your presentations or talks short, 15 to 20 minutes at the most.** If long explanations are necessary, the presentations should be broken up with practice sessions, questions, or other participatory interaction.

49

2. **Involve the students as much as possible.** Welcome questions, engage students in conversation, encourage discussion. Be sure to leave adequate time in your schedule for discussion.

3. **Use a variety of techniques.** Avoid gimmicks and fancy devices for their own sake, but integrate three to five different techniques or devices into each session. Each one breaks the monotony and keeps the group interested. Different techniques also help people learn in different ways. One person might learn from your presentation, another from a slide show, a third from drawing on a flip chart, and a fourth from the question-and-answer period.

4. **Visual aids help the learning process.** Flip charts, slides, PowerPoint and posters all add to your presentation.

Facilities have a lot to do with the success of your interaction, and some planning should be done, if possible, to make your setting as conducive as possible to learning.

Materials Preparation

Your materials must be prepared as well. Too often handouts or reading materials are an afterthought, or sometimes no thought is given to them at all. Many an administrator has had the experience of the new teacher, enthusiastic and knowledgeable, who showed up with a reading list of ten books for a short, noncredit course, unaware that most working adults cannot and will not read so much material. The opposite extreme - no handouts, no references, no directions for further learning - is just as poor.

Although each class will vary in its needs for written materials, the following are general outlines for preparing materials.

Most adults won't have time to read a whole book, but chapters or articles are feasible. Following the copyright laws, using articles or chapters is a good way to convey information without burdening the student too much.

You can prepare other handouts. This is the best way to convey most succinctly the information you deem most important. Be sure to use handouts well. Don't put down on paper things more effectively conveyed through speaking. Don't overdo handouts. Put down information participants should know or can use after the course. Use handout material for things it would take too long to copy in class, or that take up too much valuable class time.

If possible, provide a reading list of references for further research or study. For practical classes, this might be a list of people, places, or other resources.

Putting Content Online

Here are the top ways you can use the web to enhance your face-to-face class:

1. Post the course outline, bibliography, and syllabus online.
2. Provide links to useful and relevant web sites.
3. Post relevant articles online.
4. Embed or link to online videos.
5. Post your slides online.
6. Produce recorded audio of some of your lectures and post it. Especially effective is recording audio to your slides.

In fact, just about any content that can be found in an online course can also be done as a supplement or aid in the conducting of a face-to-face course as well.

Overstructuring

Although there is no such thing as over-preparing for a class, there is the definite danger of overstructuring the course or an individual class. Overstructuring is simply cramming too many things into one time period, or controlling the class session so much that the participants lose all sense of participation, involvement, and enjoyment. It is definitely not wise to structure the class session so that one or more of the following mistakes can occur:

• Every minute of the class session is scheduled.

• Too many facts, figures, and points are made within one time session without adequate breathing time, reflection, or questions. There is inadequate time for discussion.

• Preparation does not mean filling up the hour with things to say, or keeping participants running so fast with exercise, reports, and taking notes that they do not have time to absorb or interact. It takes forethought to schedule discussion, thought time, and breaks.

Chapter 7.
Building Hybrid Courses

"Isn't it great living in the future?"

— Author's son Willie talking with his friend Landon

It is time for your in-person course to be hybrid, utilizing the resources of the web. We have stated that learners in courses that incorporate online learning in some fashion learn more than people who only have traditional classroom meetings and resources.

In a few years just about every face-to-face course will be, and should be, hybrid.

Hybrid courses are sometimes called blended, mixed, flipped or web enhanced courses.[1] It doesn't matter what you call it. It means you and your learners use online resources, usually in an online classroom, for part of their study and learning. You as the teacher know your subject and your audience best, so you decide what and how much goes online.

Less class time. One of the options you have when turning your course into hybrid is to meet less frequently in-person. With hybrid, your participants can learn the same amount, even more, in fewer class meetings. In general, you can cut your class meetings by a third or even half if you want and still be able to cover everything.

Less class time is almost always welcomed by teachers and participants alike, because it means less travel time, fewer costs (e.g. babysitter, meals, parking), and the ability to schedule or reallocate that time for other professional or personal priorities and activities.

More discussion time. Most hybrid courses put some or most of the course content online. This allows you to spend more of the class time interacting with your participants.

That interaction includes, but is not limited to:

• Questions and answers

• Discussion

• Participant presentations

• Small group activities

• Helping your participants individually

• Doing assignments or work in class so that you as teacher can help your learners.

So instead of spending class time lecturing, you spend more time interacting with your learners.[2]

Time is less important online. Be aware that in the online world, how much time a learner spends online is less important than whether the person is learning. Not everyone will spend the same amount of time online. So instead of measuring time, create online quizzes for each unit of your course. You want to be more concerned about whether they are passing the unit quizzes than how much time they spend online.

An online classroom is ideal. For a hybrid course, the ideal online tool is called an online classroom or online platform. If you are teaching for an educational institution, the institution most likely already has an online classroom platform it uses. Ask, because they can set up an online classroom for you. If you are teaching solo, for a small organization, or for an organization without an online classroom platform, email your author's organization at info@lern.org (no 'a' in lern) and we can recommend several options, including the platform we use. At the time of this writing, platforms and their features and pricing change fairly frequently, so providing a list here would be out of date by the time you read this.

If there is no way you can utilize an online classroom, then consider a blog or a web site where you can utilize some (but probably not all) of the features of a hybrid course.

Take an online course. Your first step should be to take an online course yourself. It is a different, but very exciting and fun, way to learn. Pick a topic you want to learn about. After the initial awkwardness for first time online learners, you will get to know others in the course, interact with your online instructor, and quickly grow to like the format. As you learn online, you also become familiar with how online courses work.

Getting trained. If you have not taught online before, you definitely should get some a) technical training, and b) pedagogical training.

Most all organizations using an online classroom provide technical training on using them, and all online classroom platform vendors or companies provide training. Some organizations also have pedagogical training. The Learning Resources Network (LERN) at www.lern.org or www.TeachingOntheNet.org provides extensive online courses on how to teach online. You can also find there our book, *Advanced Teaching Online,* by William A. Draves, which is a fundamental and essential resource to teaching online.

Getting technical help. You may not need any technical help at all with building your hybrid course. All of the features we discuss here for online learning and teaching are already built into most all online classroom platforms. If, like this author, you have little or no technical ability, do not worry. There are numerous people who can help you with the technical stuff. Other teachers, colleagues at work, and neighbors are all possibilities. I highly recommend college students, high school students, maybe middle school students, or any other kid who suggests he or she can help you. Kids know the tech stuff and work for little money, cookies and brownies, trading homework help, and other win-win and low cost remuneration arrangements.

Where to start. The first place to start with building a hybrid course is generally with posting assignments, course information, a syllabus, and other class expectations, announcements or other information you want everyone in your course to know.

Build features one at a time. From there, you can choose any or all of the other facets of online course features. I would suggest you build your hybrid course one feature at a time. Unlike a totally online course, which has to be entirely built before it can be offered, one nice aspect of the hybrid course is that you can have just one feature online and your students can immediately benefit from that feature. Instead of trying to build too many features online at once, I would suggest you build one feature at a time, encourage your students to use it, and then begin work on the next feature. This will also give you the time and energy to improve or enhance your existing feature should you find you want to improve it before working on the next feature.

In considering which of the features of an online course to build first, or next, you would want to consider:

- Which feature will benefit my students the most.
- Which feature do my students say they would like and use the most.
- Which feature adds most to the content or subject matter of the course.
- Which feature provides the most benefit for the lowest input of time, energy and resources.

You can start anywhere, and choose any online feature at any point.

The Big Five

Here are the big five areas of online features to consider, each distinct from the others in terms of the learning benefit, and each making a different contribution to the learning process.

1. Content, not just online readings, but also simulations, webquests, animations, and videos.

2. Quizzes, especially those that provide immediate student feedback and also provide you with information on how well each student is doing. Online quizzes are an excellent way to provide frequent testing, which has proven itself to be not only an assessment tool, but an aid that improves learning as well.

3. Audio or video presentations with slides. At this level you clearly move away from the traditional classroom delivery and provide your oral presentations online in an asynchronous format, allowing your students to access them during their peak learning time. You record your best presentation, and then – except for minor changes at your discretion – you can shift your instructor time to focus more on your students and on the in-class discussions rather than repeat lectures and information transfer.

4. Online Discussions. With hybrid classes, you clearly want to utilize your in-person class meetings for discussion, student presentations, question and answers, small group discussions, and other integrative activities. But online discussions, conducted in between class meetings, may provide an additional or supplemental avenue for communication and dialogue.

Some students tend to participate more in online discussions than in-person discussions. Some topics may lend themselves to online discussion better than in-person. While online discussion in a hybrid course should, in most instances, not replace in-class communication and discussion, it may serve as a tool for you to do some things you cannot do during class time.

5. Activities and projects, including collaborative student projects as well as individual projects, which can either be done online or are posted as completed projects online.

Hybrid and Online Course Features. Within the five major areas of hybrid or online areas of features, here are some of the features you can find, and you can build, into your hybrid course.

Information

Readings. Information you want your participants to read in preparation for your class meetings. These can be either original material you have written, or articles available on the web.

Web sites. Links to web sites with relevant information.

References. Supplemental readings, including books and other references you want your participants to know about for further study.

Announcements. Information about your class.

Calendar updates. Meeting date changes, location changes, and other news.

Assignments. Work your participants need to do during the course.

Content

Audio. Clips of famous speeches, music, and radio programs

Virtual Tours. Your participants visit a series of web sites on the same theme or subject.

WebQuests. With a WebQuest, your participants not only go to several different web sites, but they engage in an activity with a stated end result during and after visiting the web sites.

Video. Video clips from history, current events, movies, and documentaries

Animations. Illustrated art or images set to motion.

Simulations. Participants model an activity online, helping to prepare for a "real world" experience or skill.

Drag-and-drop exercises. A form of simulation where the participant moves the cursor to complete an activity, enhancing their learning by the physical movement and engagement with the cursor.

Quizzes, games and puzzles. From Jeopardy style games and multiple-choice quizzes to more sophisticated online games and puzzles, games increase the learning by making the task both challenging and fun.

Audio lectures. You record and post your audio lectures on the web. Slides accompany the audio.

Interactivity

Homework via email. If your participants do assignments or homework, have them submit it to you via email or posting it on the web.

Grades online. If you are doing a formal or credit course, there is software to post grades and scores online so an individual student can see his or her progress.

Self-Quizzes. Regardless of the type of course you are teaching, people learn more when they can take self-quizzes. Self-quizzes are usually multiple choice, short, and the computer automatically grades them and tells the learner the results immediately.

Collaborative projects. A collaborative project is one in which your participants work in small groups on a common project, such as an essay, WebQuest, or presentation.

Online presentations. Online presentations can be done either individually or by a small group. Online presentations include slide presentations, role playing, online debates, and other activities.

Discussion and Assessment

Asynchronous Discussions. Online class discussions take place continually. Anyone can post a comment anytime, which is called an asynchronous discussion, and others can respond anytime.

Tests and Assessments. A variety of tests and assessments can be created to evaluate your participants' learning.

You begin building your hybrid course with one of the above features that has the greatest impact at the lowest input of time, energy and resources. And as you become more experienced as a hybrid instructor, you want to move to moving your lectures and presentations online. When you put your presentations online, that is a turning point that moves you, your teaching, and your course to a whole new level of maximizing both online resources and the in-person environment.

If you are teaching a face-to-face class and interested in using the web to make your course hybrid, our book *Advanced Teaching Online* is equally relevant to the hybrid situation and the totally online course.

Chapter 8.
Discovering Your Participants

"And then you make them believe."

— Jerold Apps, well-known adult educator

There are four things you as a teacher of adults must do to have a successful teaching experience. I have developed the schematic **DIVE** to elaborate on them, as in "dive or plunge into your teaching." The next four chapters are devoted to the four critical aspects of the DIVE approach.

The first letter in DIVE stands for Discover your participants.

Finding Out Who Your Participants Are

As soon as you can, find out who your participants are. Ask the institution sponsoring your course about who usually registers. Before the first class, talk to as many participants as possible. During the first class, you may want to spend a little time discussing past experiences and hobbies. After class or between classes, continue learning about the participants.

Participant diversity is one of the greater assets your course can have, but to use it properly, you have to know it exists. Knowing who your participants are is essential.

Meeting Participant Expectations

Find out what your participants expect from your class. The success of the class depends on meeting their needs. Although you as the teacher may feel their hopes are obvious-learning the subject you are offering-that may not be the whole story.

By being flexible enough to meet different intentions, you can improve the class. That may mean taking a break in the middle of the class to serve refreshments, encouraging people to meet afterward at Joe's Bar, or spending a session talking about job opportunities in your field of study. By adjusting your agenda slightly to meet those wishes, you will find a more enthusiastic group of individuals in your class.

Here are some questions to ask your participants individually or in a group. The answers will serve as tip-offs to what they anticipate, and also what they might contribute to the group.

- Have you studied this topic before?
- Why did you decide to take this course?
- Have you had any experience or work in this area before?
- What would you like to do with this course after you are finished?
- What is your work?
- What would you like to be doing in two years?
- How did you hear about this course?

The First Class

The first class is important. In fact, it is not overstating to say it is critical to the success of your course. Your participants arrive, often as individuals who do not know each other. And they have some anxiety, some fear, of not knowing whether they will fit in, be able to master the subject, enjoy it, be humiliated, be frustrated, be bored, or whether the adult learning situation will be too hard for them.

And from that unrelated, anxious, skeptical gathering of individuals, you as the teacher have to pull it all together: make them a group, get them to know one another, establish a relationship with them, excite them about the subject they will be learning, and encourage them to return for the next time.

As one participant remembers, "It was three times as scary." The participant recalled his first night in a cardiopulmonary resuscitation (CPR) class with teacher Jim Frandy at the Lakeland Elementary School in Manitowash Waters, Wisconsin.

"It was scary because I didn't know any of the other students, and quite frankly, they were a little different from me. It was scary because the subject was death, and how I might, or worse, might not, save someone's life. And it was scary because the teacher was telling us we would have to take a test at the end of the course.

"But Mr. Frandy made everyone so at ease almost immediately. He was very reassuring. He told us who he was, asked us why we were there, and he told us to relax. That was easy because he was relaxed.

"He also told us something very important about himself, that he once had to use CPR, and although he did it correctly, the man died. I don't know why, but that made it less scary as well, to know something of him, and also to know that sometimes, even if you do it correctly, a person can still die."

Making that first class a success is still a tall order, but one that can be achieved. And the satisfaction of having achieved a cohesive group interested in your subject after one meeting is worth the effort. And you will have help. Some of the participants will have taken courses before, and will be much more at ease. Others will have had some contact with or knowledge of the subject and be willing to share their experience and excitement about the topic with the rest of the class. You also will have a class plan, and that scheme of introducing activities for the first class also will help you through.

The foremost adult educator in the country, Malcolm Knowles, tells about his own first class.

The foremost adult educator in the country in the last century, Malcolm Knowles, tells about his own first class.

"The opening session, the opening hour or two or three in any activity is the most single critical time of the whole period in which I engage learners. It is at this time that we become acquainted with each other. It is during this time we survey the resources the students are bringing to the class. It is during this time we build a collaborative rather than a competitive relationship among the students in the group. We build an atmosphere of mutual trust, mutual respect, supportiveness, and I present myself as a human being. I also explain my role as a facilitator and resource person, and what theoretical framework underlies the approach I use. I tell them I am a trout fisherman from Montana."[1]

What should happen

Here's what should happen during the first class.

1. You should get to know the students, as many as possible.

2. You should introduce yourself, and establish your humanness.

3. The participants should be introduced to each other.

4. You should eliminate any fear or anxiety by providing a relaxing and informal activity.

5. Participants should be immediately invited to participate, most commonly by having them tell a little about themselves.

6. The subject should be introduced as well as what the course will cover.

7. The style of your teaching should be established and your techniques described to eliminate any fears of a boring class.

8. The participants should become involved in the course in some way.

9. You should encourage your participants' return by describing what they can expect next time.

10. You should try to get any preliminary feedback from participants at the close of the class or afterward.

11. You should internally review the class session, what went well, what could have been done better, what you can do next time.

Preparing for the First Class

Although each class meeting needs preparation, your first class will differ from all of the other meetings. For that reason, you should design a special preparation worksheet just for the first class to accomplish all of the tasks, activities, and atmosphere setting required for the first meeting.

Here is a sample worksheet covering all of the aspects of the first class.

Activity	*Method*	*Materials*	*Time*
1. Welcome			
2. Introducing Myself			
3. Participants' Introductions			
4. Ice-Breaker			
5. Assessing Learner Needs (Why did you come?)			

6. Announcements

7. Introduction of Subject/Topic

8. Break

9. Participant Involvement

10. Summary

11. Personal Evaluation of First Session

The second step to your participation is to go through each stage of the first session mentally and envision what will take place and how. This will give you a familiarity with the first class, so that when you actually do it, you will be more comfortable because you will have already done it before in your mind. It also will give you a chance to go through your checklist of activities, methods, materials, and times to make sure everything is in order, and that you have not forgotten something needed for the class. For example, for coffee break, do I have cups, sugar, coffeemaker, and so on?

The third step in your preparation is rehearsing. By knowing your material well, you will establish confidence in your participants about you as an instructor. On the first meeting, you should have it all together. This doesn't mean memorizing, and it certainly does not mean reading a speech or lacking spontaneity. But it does mean knowing your material fully and having everything in place — your notes, materials, instructional aids, and your thoughts — opening, topic in proper sequence, summary, and closing.

Teachers, even those who have taught previous classes, are just as susceptible to little nervous jitters as the participants. Jane Vella, in her book *Training Through Dialogue,* reveals, "I personally always get 'butterflies' before a course begins. It's nature's way, as I see it, to keep me aware of the responsibility I have to learners, and to the program, and to myself." She also suggests allowing yourself some quiet time before a class begins to try to alleviate some of the nervousness that can be very visible to your students.[2]

The First Class — Step by Step

Let's go through that first class meeting, step by step.

1. Arrive early, well in advance of the class starting time, and before any participants are likely to arrive. Have the room or building "ready" by the time the students come. When the participants come in, they will feel welcome and the atmosphere will be set so you can spend time with them.

2. As each student arrives, greet him or her at the door.

3. Spend some pre-class time with the participants. By now, your notes should be in order, and you should not be reviewing your materials, but getting to know your students. Break down some initial barriers and engage in small talk. Get to know, as best you can, some of the students. Find out if anyone has had previous experience with the topic, why they came, how they heard about the class, and so on. This pre-class chatter not only makes the participants more comfortable, but also provides you with noteworthy examples to use when the class gets going.

4. Just before the class begins, do two things. Take a few deep breaths and relax. And two, make sure you are enjoying all this!

5. Welcome participants to the class. Acknowledge the effort they are making to add the class to an already hectic schedule. Express appreciation for that effort and for their interest in your subject.

6. Introduce yourself. Participants are interested in knowing two things about an instructor. The first is that he or she is "qualified" to teach. Those qualifications are almost always viewed as experience or competence in the subject, not in terms of academic schooling or degrees obtained.

Students want to know you are their "superior" in the subject about which they are to learn, but they also want to know you are a peer in every other way. So you also want to establish a relationship with your participants that indicates some of your personal, though not necessarily private, characteristics. "And then you make them believe," says Jerry Apps.[3]

7. The participants introduce themselves. It is important for the participants to know each other and to be involved in the class as soon as possible. Introductions are the first opportunity to involve each person in the class, and that early involvement will help keep the person interested throughout the class. Have all participants introduce themselves even if everyone knows everyone else.

Malcolm Knowles outlines this exercise for helping to establish a climate for learning. Ask the participants to share the following information about themselves:

- What they are, relating their present work roles and past experience;
- Who they are, sharing one thing about themselves that will enable oth-

ers to see them as unique human beings, different from everyone else
in the room;

• Any special resources they bring with them that are relevant to this
course or workshop;

• And any questions, problems, or concerns they have about the unique
characteristics of adults as learners about taking responsibility for
their own learning.[4]

8. Help establish a learning climate, an atmosphere of trust and friend-
liness —and the feeling of security on the part of each adult learner is a vital
prerequisite to that person's learning anything in your class.

9. Assess the needs of your learners. Each person in the class, of course,
will have individual needs and wishes, and your one group session will not be
able to meet every need of every student in the class. But you can make the
class more meaningful and successful to them by trying to meet as many of
their needs as possible. In assessing what your participants want out of your
class, you may find that:

• A few expected something different from the class, and that you can,
in these early stages, revise your course outline to meet their needs.

• Several individuals may want more emphasis or additional material
in certain areas. Throughout the course you can spend some time
meeting those individual wishes by devoting a few more minutes on a
particular area, or adding comments specifically because of a request.

• One or more individuals may be coming to the wrong class and they
may wish to look elsewhere for the kind of learning they are seeking.

The advantage of finding out what your participants want to learn is
twofold: you learn what they want and are more apt to provide the kind of
learning that will satisfy the most learners; and they understand more clearly
why they are in the class, and are better able to benefit and evaluate their own
experience based on a clearer idea of what they expected.

Many teachers assess learner needs by simply going around the class and
asking participants to express why they came and what they hope to learn.
Another way to do it is to play a game or do an exercise that will bring out the
students' expectations.

And finally, some teachers introduce the subject and then at the end of the first class meeting ask for student responses and changes in the course outline. The result is usually more satisfied learners, a happier teacher, and more learning taking place.

10. Make any announcements and get any housekeeping tasks out of the way before you get into the subject of the course.

11. Introduce the subject. This may mean going over your course outline. It may mean getting your feet wet in the topic area but saving the full plunge for the second class. Or it may mean jumping right in and taking off. It is important, however, that the students leave with some new piece of information or knowledge after the first session. You need to sell your students not just on the subject matter but on your teaching as well. So use different techniques, involve the students as much as possible, and make the presentation interesting, lively, and diverse.

12. If your class lasts more than an hour, be sure to plan a break. Breaks are not just wasted time. They are important for adults to recoup their energy and attention, to recap a little of what they have learned, and to know the other participants better. Although a break may just be a break for the students, it is often an excellent opportunity for the teacher to learn about the students.

13. At the end of the first class, you will want to summarize what they have learned, to point out, possibly in a subtle way, what they have achieved, and in this way, give them something to take back home. You also need to get them excited about returning, and stimulate their interest further in the course. As Jane Vella says, "The first day, and all days, end with some form of closure as well. A simple thank you for your hard work may be used, or a preview of day two. Closure is essential. It is a way of respecting the learners."[5]

14. Be available for five to twenty minutes of informal contact with the participants after the end of the class meeting. But British educator Ralph Ruddock warns, "Beware of being captured by a pub-group, sub-group, or tea-group. That demotes other members."[6]

Being overly familiar or attentive to any one person or section of the class can be discouraging to others.

15. Immediately after the class is over, take a few moments to reflect and relive it. What went well? What didn't go well? What could be improved for next time? What should be changed for next time?

The first session is critical for the success of your course. It is a tough task to accomplish all of the things that need to be done in that first hour or so. By having done it, you should be able to look back on it and say not only that you survived the first class, but also that it was a good experience as well.

Icebreakers

Icebreakers are techniques used at the beginning of the first class to reduce tension and anxiety, to acquaint participants with each other, to immediately involve the class members.

Use one or more as you see fit. Don't be afraid to experiment and try a different approach, but use an icebreaker because you want to, not as a time-filler or because an outline says it should be used. Be creative and design your own variations.

Here are ten types of icebreakers and some variations.

Introduce myself. Participants introduce themselves and tell why they are there. Variations: Participants tell where they first heard about the class, how they became interested in the subject, their occupation, hometown, favorite television program, or the best book they have read in the past year.

Introduce another. Divide the class into pairs. Each person talks about himself or herself to the other, sometimes with specific instructions to share a piece of information. For example, "The one thing I fear the most is..." or "One thing I am particularly proud of is..." After five minutes, the partici-pants introduce the other person to the rest of the class. Variations: Have each person write some thing on a blank index card, pass out the cards, and have people find each other first before making the introductions.

Character descriptions. Have people write one to three adjectives describing themselves on a blank index card. Put these on a stick-on badge. Have class members find someone with similar or opposite adjectives and talk for five minutes with the other person. Variations: Have each person think up an adjective describing himself, such as "Hopeful Sue"; have an adjective start with the same letter as the name, such as "Roaming Robert"; relate favorite food, wine, color, famous person; "If I were a food, I would be "_____; "If I were an affliction, I would be a _____, because _____

Find someone. Each person writes on a blank index card one to three statements, such as favorite color, interests, hobbies, or vacation. Pass out the cards so everyone gets someone else's card. Have people find the person with their card and introduce themselves. Variations: write down a fact, such as occupation, age, high school, or home state.

Guess. Play "What's my line?" and have class members guess each person's occupation. Variations: home state, neighborhood, make of car.

Get to know an object. Bring a bag of potatoes to class. Give each person a potato. Have everyone "get to know" the potato, and then introduce the potato to another person, or to the rest of the class. Throw all the potatoes into a pile and have the participants find their own potato. Variations: fruit, such as a pear, that people can eat afterward; get to know a shoe, introduce it, throw it in a pile and blindfolded, find your shoe.

Physical introductions. With eyes closed, everyone walks around the room shaking hands and saying hello to the others. Variations: with eyes open, participants go around and introduce their backs to every other person's back in the class; divide into pairs, one person closes his fist and the other tries to get it open; bumper cars - - hands at the sides, eyes closed, students walk around until they bump into someone, then introduce themselves, and keep moving; introduce their feet to someone else, usually with everyone on his back on the floor.

Fantasies. People write a famous name on a piece of paper and pin it on someone else's back. That person tries to guess what name is pinned on his own back. Variations: person acts or talks like his fantasy person while class or one other person tries to guess the person; participants talk about their fantasy person and why they admire the person or would like to be the fantasy person.

Word associations. Ask your participants to write down what comes to mind when they hear the word "renaissance," or some other word. Then ask them to share the thoughts with another person. Variations: use a word that introduces the subject matter; do the association game orally.

Group exercise. Divide the class into several groups. Hand out puzzle pieces and have each group together try to put the puzzle in order. Variations: some of the puzzle pieces are in another group, and groups have to trade for one or two of the pieces. Create something. Divide into groups and pass out ordinary office supplies or objects to each group (like pencils, paper clips, or rubber bands). Ask each group to discuss, manipulate, and create a design of human nature with the objects. Have groups look at the other designs and explain the symbolism. Variations: create a design with tinker toys, playing cards, watercolors, or crayons.

Chapter 9.
Involving Your Participants

"To know how to suggest is the art of teaching."

— Amiel, 19th Century Swiss Philosopher

The most dynamic and variable element in your adult teaching situation will be the participants themselves. Working with this resource is both a challenge and an opportunity to make your class exciting. You can unearth potential, ideas, and interaction you and they probably did not know exist.

Expectations are central to tapping your human resources. It is important for you to know who your participants are, what they expect from the class, why some of them may drop out, what they can and want to contribute, and how to adjust to their differing expectations.

Thus, the second key point in the DIVE approach to teaching adults is to Involve your participants.

Students As Participants

Probably the greatest resource for your class and your teaching will be the participants themselves. Unlike a formal educational classroom where students are not perceived to have much knowledge in the subject, you will find your participants have skills, talents, and perspectives you can and should use in the course.

Your learning situation will differ from a traditional classroom. There will be many kinds of people with different backgrounds. That variety can be turned into an exciting learning process by playing on the worldliness of the

73

people in the group. Every person in the group has had some life adventures, and just as important, relates to what you are discussing from his or her own perspective. By using the group members' own experiences, the teacher can involve them in the learning process to a much greater degree than if the teacher only used his or her own situation, or merely asked for the members' opinions.

Tapping the knowledge of your participants has at least three benefits. First, being involved enhances their learning. Second, their feedback and interaction can substantiate your input and be a good teaching aid for your points. And third, they will come up with some facts, information, or ideas you hadn't considered.

Do not make the mistake of being too apprehensive about your participants' knowledge. Too many teachers are defensive or condescending about their students' comprehension. They try to avoid student input, seek to establish their superior wisdom, or try to correct students needlessly. These reactions may come from a false impression about what the teacher is and is not supposed to do. You are not supposed to know everything about the subject, and the students are not presumed to understand little or nothing about the subject. You can learn as much as the students and you can learn from the students. The students do not expect you to possess complete wisdom. Your participants' impressions, whether correct or whether totally misinformed, are important to them, and just as critical to you the teacher if you are to help them learn "the true way" and obtain more enlightened information or skills.

Students respect a teacher more for admitting less-than-Zeus-like competence in the subject area. They know no one has a monopoly on any subject.

Teachers must deal with two general kinds of training students bring to class. The first is genuine information and skills, and you should recognize, praise, and use that talent in your class. The second is misinformation resulting from inadequate or less-than-satisfactory previous learning. Instead of attacking that inadequate information, the teacher can point to the one or two correct statements the student is making and elaborate on them, or use the student in examples demonstrating your information.

A teacher may even find someone in the class more knowledgeable than he or she. One science fiction enthusiast, who had studied and read and written science fiction for years, offered a class on the subject. When the class met, the teacher was surprised to find out that everyone not only had a good deal of knowledge in science fiction, but also had published a work of science fiction ... every one, that is, except the teacher. Instead of giving up or being resentful, he used their experience and they used his, and they all learned from each other.

Ways to Involve Learners

Here are ways to involve learners, including tapping your participants' skills and knowledge.

Questions. Encourage questions from your participants.

Experiences. Ask your participants for experiences relating to the topic you are discussing.

Bring examples. Have your learners bring to class examples pertaining to the subject.

Discussion. Divide into groups for discussion.

Leaders. Have one or more students lead the class for a portion of a meeting, serve as recorder, and/or discussion leaders.

Pair up. Divide the class into pairs and have the participants share an experience with each other.

Bring music. Each class meeting, invite a different participant to bring in music to play before class time or during a break.

Presentations. Take turns having participants give presentations.

Peer review. Have learners evaluate each other, grading tests and providing feedback on group activities.

Tutoring. Peer teaching works. Have participants serve as mentors or tutors for each other.

Buddies. Pair up to provide emotional support, encouragement, and sharing.

Study groups. For reviewing course material or preparing for an exam.

Group projects. Learners engage in activities and out-of-class projects together.

The Teachable Moment

One of the more elusive, rarely discussed, and exhilarating experiences is "the teachable moment." It is one of the more difficult situations for the teacher to handle, mainly as it comes without warning and because it requires the teacher to relinquish control of the class. The sociologist Havighurst first defined "the teachable moment" in 1947 as a time in one's life when one is ready to learn, and is eager and able to absorb what the teacher has to offer. It can be a time in life, but it can also be a time during the class session when students suddenly perk up.

Many teachers have had the experience. One is teaching, and then someone says something and a mental bell rings, eyes light up, heads turn, ears tune in, and the entire class is suddenly alive. It is an exhilarating time that may last for seconds or minutes, yet a time when a word or gesture from you as a teacher may mean more than the rest of the hour, or sometimes the whole course. It is a moment that has been defined and shaped not by the teacher, but by the participants. They have caught onto something, and whether it is a comment from the teacher, or just as likely, a comment from another partici-pant, the learners have defined their interest and made this learning moment theirs. The teachable moment is really a peak learning moment because now is not the time to lecture or talk, but to respond to the participants. It is the time to try to enhance and extend that peak learning moment.

For the teacher, it is a difficult time. Your first response as a teacher is to try to regain control. You may try to limit discussion because time is running out, and move on to your next point. Or you may try to interject and use the moment to convey your most important ideas. But those responses usually just inhibit or cut short the learning moment.

The learning moment is the learner's moment, and the best help the teacher can provide is to let go, allowing the learners to set the agenda and direct the conversation. Your most valuable contribution is simply to have created the environment. If you can recognize that magical moment, let it happen, and flow with it, you will participate in one of the more rewarding experiences of being a teacher, "the teachable moment."

Dropouts

Every teacher should expect people to drop out of class. Whether this has a debilitating effect or is expected often means the difference between whether the class is perceived as a success or a failure.

One factor contributing to the dropout rate is the fact that the criteria for a voluntary class are so much higher than for a more traditional school class. The participants want their time to be used wisely and are sensitive to class sessions of low quality. Because it is so easy for participants to walk out or just not show up the next time, each class has to be rewarding to attract the participants to return.

Some people will discover they know much of what is being discussed. Others will find the topic is not quite what they had expected. A few may have to leave because of extenuating circumstances such as illness, work responsibilities, or family.

Other less-legitimate reasons for dropping out of a class include lack of interest and lack of self-discipline. These, of course, are not under the control of the teacher and are hard to combat. A few words at the beginning of the course about responsibility to the group might be helpful.

Whether one person drops out or half the group leaves, the teacher should not let this hinder the class in any way. If you expect some people to drop out and don't attribute this to your own abilities as a teacher, you can concentrate on those who remain in the group.

Adjusting to Differing Expectations

Sometimes the expectations of one or more students will differ from yours. This is a difficult situation but one that cannot be ignored. The best way to deal with differing expectations is to get them out front and clearly defined.

- What do you want?
- What do I want?
- What is going on now?
- And how can we work it out to our mutual satisfaction?

If it is an individual or two, you can talk to them and work out something that does not redirect the entire class. You could spend part of a class addressing their special interests. You could spend time after the class on their particular needs or interests. Or you could suggest resources for them to explore their interest independently. If more than just a few have differing expectations, you should reevaluate the course. Perhaps you can change the course, perhaps they can be enthusiastic about your direction for the class, or perhaps you can design a class for later.

Part of the joy of teaching adults is interacting with and exploring the skills, talents, and ideas of your participants. Although the diverse perspectives and unexpected feedback may occasionally challenge your facilitating abilities, the overall outcome is a creative and productive interaction that is rewarding to participants and teacher alike.

Emailing or Texting Participants

Email represents a great way for you to communicate briefly and quickly with your participants between class meetings, keeping them more involved in your course. Participants born after 1980 may prefer to communicate via text, so ask them their preferred way to communicate.

There are several good uses of email and/or texting.

Upcoming class notice. A day or two before the next class, send a short email to your class participants. Each email notice should have two parts: a) Topic or theme of the next class meeting to get them looking forward to the new material; and b) Words of encouragement or praise, such as "The course is going great!" or "Good discussion last meeting."

Again, the email should be very short to increase readability and generate interest. Also, it is best if you send out your upcoming class email notice the same day of the week each time, even the same time of day. That creates familiarity, and people will anticipate your email notice.

Personal communication. If an individual has a private issue or circumstance, email is a good way to discuss it with you.

Answer questions. If you want to answer questions in between class meetings, let your class members know. If you respond to an individual's question, remember that others in the class have not received that additional information. If everyone agrees, you can include all members in the class on each email response.

If the questions and answers become very numerous, roughly more than one a day, you should consider switching from email to an asynchronous online discussion board to dialogue online between class meetings. The asynchronous online discussion board is the best way to engage your participants in dialogue.

You can also set limits on what days or times you can respond to email questions. If you are not available certain days, such as weekends, just let your class members know in advance what times you will be responding to questions.

Where to place email addresses. There are several reasons why you should put the email addresses of your participants in the BCC: area. You may want to keep your participants' email addresses private and not distribute the addresses to everyone in the class. To ensure the privacy of your learners' email addresses, send your emails to yourself and put your class members' email addresses in the BCC: area where they cannot be seen by others in the class. Another reason to put participant emails in the BCC: area is that they take up visual space in another location, especially if you have a large class. Taking up visual space means they distract from your message.

In addition to participation being a good process technique, using the students as participants will increase the learning. The more they are involved in a group, the better people learn. People will also learn by listening to and interacting with other group members. The teacher often learns from the participants who may offer different views on the subject. If the teacher spends less time in solo performances, and the participants are involved in the group, people will be attentive and the learning will be enhanced.

Chapter 10.
Varying Your Teaching Techniques

"Not all learning comes from books. You have to live a lot."

Loretta Lynn, country-western singer

There is no best teaching technique to use in teaching adults. The only bad technique is the one that is used repeatedly with the same group. What is important is to try several new ideas every time you teach. As in everything else, some of them will not work while others will be a surprising success. But it is that variety in teaching techniques which enables adults to learn. The experimentation will also keep you interested in each class. Thus, the third key point in the DIVE approach to teaching adults is to Vary your teaching techniques.

These suggestions are like ingredients for a stew. Mix them as you wish, and be sure to add your own special flavoring to the pot to make it unique to you.

Modes of Teaching

For the adult-oriented teaching you will be doing, there are basically four types of learning formats, depending on what kind of subject you are teaching. Each one is designed to gain maximum involvement from the participants and be as attractive a process as possible. You should choose your format and then elaborate upon it, using some techniques to enhance the

81

model. Sometimes it is possible to use two or more modalities for one class, but usually the modality is restricted by your choice of subject.

Group Discussion. The group discussion has replaced the formal classroom procedure as the most common format for adult learning. It is generally used for idea-related topics, including current events, philosophy and personal growth, as well as academic subjects involving reading and discussion.

To prevent the situation from dissolving into a bull session, the teacher should introduce new subject material each meeting in an informal talk. Uninterrupted lecturing or one-way communicative styles should be avoided at all times. The group discussion is usually located in an informal environment, such as a living room, with people seated so that they are able to see and respond to others. If the people introduce themselves at the beginning of the class, they will feel more open about contributing remarks and comments.

In the group discussion format, the teacher needs to develop creative ways of introducing material to the group, and has to be attentive to involving the members in discussion. Knowledge of group process, facilitating, and group dynamics helps this format. The creative use of reading materials is problematic. Books and articles are often burdening to people who have little extra time for reading. Assigning one or two articles or a chapter of a book is one solution.

Over-the-Shoulder Demonstration. The over-the-shoulder demonstration format is most often used with practical skills classes, such as small appliance repair, carpentry, and auto mechanics. The attractiveness of this format is that it brings into the learning situation the material about which the group is talking.

The location of the class should be in a room free of furniture that might be in the way. A church basement or meeting room is appropriate. The teacher starts by talking about a particular aspect of the topic, and then moves quickly from talking to doing, for example, fixing a lamp while the class looks on. It is important that people be as close as possible to the action, so they can ask questions and discuss what is happening while the teacher is demonstrating. Then, depending on the resources available, the teacher can guide the participants as they perform the activity just demonstrated.

Sometimes a "chalk talk," or using an easel for making a point enables the teacher to add theoretical points or ideas to the demonstration. Though seemingly simple, it is important with this model (as with others) to plan objectives for each session. The format stays away from book-learning and concentrates on the tangible, the concrete, thus making it a captivating format.

Show-and-Do Involvement. Unlike the others, the show-and-do format revolves around the participants rather than the teacher. It is most often used in arts and crafts kinds of classes where each participant is to create or build something individually. Examples of the format are painting, drawing, chess, and weaving.

The method is the most involving, with each participant doing or learning while the teacher demonstrates. The teacher interjects new ideas or suggestions by interrupting the group and introducing a new idea at once.

A variation on this is to take the group out of the classroom and into the setting where the activity takes place, such as using a lake for sailing instruction or a garage for auto mechanics.

Formal Classroom Instruction. At times, a formal classroom setting is most appropriate for learning. Generally, the formal setting — a room geared for learning rather than relaxing, with the desks or chairs arranged to give the teacher maximum attention and authority, and a rather traditional approach to instruction—is inappropriate for adults who do not want credits or job skills. But for those situations and others, a classroom setting may get results. Basic education classes, such as writing and mathematics, or job skills classes such as typing or shorthand are examples. Traditional approaches, individualized instruction, and other methods can be explored here.

Project Format. One final format should be mentioned, and that is the project format. Projects are simply learning and doing situations in which the class works to produce something while they are learning. The advantages of this style of learning are twofold: 1) the group learns by doing, an acknowledged learning method, and 2) the people in the group gain a sense of accomplishment. Examples of classes in which the project method would be useful are dome building and community power structures. The first class would actually build a dome while the second group would research their town and write a report on their community's power structure.

Leading a Discussion

If there is any teaching method to be favored over all the others, it is probably the group discussion. The group discussion lends itself particularly well to adults. It can be used in most any type of class and can be adapted to any teaching format, whether you are using the discussion, demonstration, how-to, or formal classroom mode of teaching.

Discussion is a good teaching method for several reasons. It is good for setting the climate, and fostering warmth, rapport, and interest among people in the group. It produces interaction among learners and motivates them to inquire further into the subject. It is also a form of feedback on their progress, and serves as a non-threatening way for adults to test their knowledge.

Confining a good discussion to just one hour is difficult. The optimal length is from one to two hours, with a break if needed. More than two hours is probably too much, less than an hour is probably too little for a discussion to reach fruition. If you have less than one hour, you can still conduct a discussion, but it will need to be more directed, involve you more as the initiator, and less should be expected from the abbreviated discussion.

Discussion tips. Here are some suggestions in designing and facilitating a discussion.

- Arrange the group in a circle.

- Have everyone, including yourself, seated.

- Don't make any speeches.

- Allow 15 minutes for the discussion to get under way. -Set a clearly defined question before the group. Sometimes it helps if the initial question is set in personal terms. For example, don't ask the group to define conservatism'. Ask, "Are you a conservative?"

- Keep the discussion on track. Try to limit your participation to areas that are important or overlooked, but assume responsibility for the direction of the discussion.

- Take time every once in a while to draw loose ends together.

- Give a sense of progress or satisfaction with the discussion, add a "shape" or "contour" to it so participants can see what they have achieved, and end on a positive note.

- Close the discussion with a summary and compliments to the participants for a job well done.

Perhaps the most difficult job in facilitating a discussion is dealing with the vocal individuals at both ends of the scale: the loud, talkative, or disruptive ones, and the quiet, inhibited, and passive folks. The approach to each type differs.

Too vocal. Those who have too much to say and are preventing others from participating should be dealt with firmly and frankly. You should be polite, with the courtesy probably diminishing if your friendly suggestions are not heeded.

Here are some phrases to use.

• "Frank, we've appreciated your comments. Now let us hear what the others have to say."

• "Shirley, why don't we give Pat, Anne, and some of the others a chance to say something?"

For a discussion to succeed, no one person should dominate it, and whatever measures are necessary to accomplish that objective should be used, including asking the disruptive person to leave if all else fails.

Reluctant. Quite another tack needs to bring out someone who is quiet, shy, reserved, or not use to talking in a group. Here you need to be subtle and delicate in your efforts. Many of the best discussion leaders adhere to one of the "bill of rights" in discussions: the right to remain silent. Pestering or annoying people into talking will not achieve their or the group's goals, and some people truly prefer to be silent. But many others are simply inhibited and appreciate being drawn into the discussion.

You can tell after one or two overtures which persons are responding and which ones are not.

Here are some techniques to bring people into the discussion.

• Don't single out an individual as the quiet one, or make a point of turning the group's attention to the individual. Instead, ask a number of people for their opinion, including the person you are trying to bring out.

• Turn to the quiet person for a response.

• Try to involve the quiet person at first in a starter question, like a response, yes or no answer, or personal opinion, rather than asking a difficult or risk-taking question for openers. Some examples: "Brenda, what do you think of what Kent just said?" "Andrew, would you agree or disagree with that?" "Paul, do you personally think media news is slanted these days?"

- Give a light, quick compliment to the person you are trying to bring out after a response. "Thank you," "Good ...," and "Interesting point," are all non-elaborate yet encouraging words. Not every discussion is perfect. Not every group will come up with an astonishing new theory or invention worth patenting. But discussions do work. Their effect is both immediate and long-term. You probably won't be aware of all the benefits taking place, yet the time and energy you put into leading a discussion is the epitome of what learning is all about: sharing.

Online Discussion

You can also have discussion between classes using your online classroom. Online, everyone can talk, and everyone can talk at the same time. You may also find some of your participants more willing to make comments online than in the classroom.

The asynchronous discussion board has been proven to be an excellent format for online discussion. Online, your participants can post a written comment anytime day or night. You check the online discussion anywhere from two times a week to daily, depending on your subject and how many people are in your class.

While most online classrooms also have the technical capacity to do live synchronous or real-time chats, the experience of almost all teachers is that only about a third to half of your participants will show up at a certain time to chat, and that the asynchronous online discussion board enables learners to make more thoughtful and in-depth comments and responses.

Like in-person discussion, online discussion doesn't just happen spontaneously. You will want to pose the first comment for the discussion each unit, and you will want to praise and encourage just like you do in-person. You do not need to reply to every comment, but you will want to post periodically, maybe two to three times a week, to make sure your participants know you are there online and engaged.

If you want to learn more about conducting online discussions, first see the chapters on it in "*Advanced Teaching Online.*" If you want a more comprehensive and intensive work, the best book is "*Continual Engagement: Fostering Online Discussion,* by Mary Dereshiwsky, also available from LERN at www.TeachingOnTheNet.org or www.lern.org.

Making Presentations

The essence of a good class presentation is not what you say but how you say it. This is not to detract from the content of what you have to offer. It is simply a recognition that adults will remember more, and learn more, if you say what you have to clearly and methodically.

Presentation style is important. A magazine once conducted a survey on how much students remembered from a psychology class. First they had a psychology professor teach a class, and then an actor who had little or no knowledge of psychology. The students remembered more of what the actor said than what the professor said. Fortunately, you don't have to be an actor to make a good presentation, but some of the techniques are similar, like timing, a good opening and closing, and knowing when to stop.

The first thing to remember in making a presentation is not to think of it as a lecture. The lecture, even a good lecture, with its podium, lifeless notes, lack of interaction, concentration on subject matter regardless of the type or size of an audience, is not a model for designing a presentation for adults. Instead, think in terms of discourse, talking, or conversation. A conversation is fresh every time, has plenty of interaction, concentrates on the listener as much as the content of what is being said, and is a much better model for constructing a presentation. Some may immediately associate conversations with rambling, talking too long, changing the subject, and being disorganized. But these are poor conversational practices that also make presentations ineffective.

Presentation length. The second most important thing about presentations is that they are rarely too short, and often too long. Educator Steven Brookfield notes, "The average attention span for listening to an uninterrupted lecture has been estimated somewhere between twelve and twenty minutes, and it is a good idea to pace your presentation what that in mind."[1] Talking too long is probably the most common error in making presentations, and can damage an otherwise excellent presentation. Keeping an imperfect presentation short can improve it in the minds of your listeners.

As one elderly Muppet told the other one from their balcony seats, "I like that last number."

"Oh, what did you like about it?"

"It was the last number."

So, too, are adults appreciative of talks that end on time. It is better to leave your audience hungry for more than to leave them wishing there was less.

The three aspects to be concerned about in making a good presentation are content, preparation and delivery.

In thinking about the content of your presentation, determine what is relevant and important and concentrate on that. Try to reduce or eliminate any other points which may be irrelevant, confusing, not important to know, or might even contradict what you are trying to convey.

The content needs to be geared to your audience's degree of familiarity. Your presentation should not be over their heads, nor should it be condescendingly basic if your listeners are already past that point. Determine as best you can the level of comprehension your audience will have.

Presentation preparation. Preparing your presentation should be similar to preparing for each class session. There should be three parts to your presentation: 1) the introduction, in which you outline what you think you will talk about; 2) the main body of the presentation; and 3) the ending, including a summary covering the most important aspects of your talk. It is not a poor practice to repeat the most significant points. In fact, it is a better practice if you can say the same thing differently each time.

When one backwoods orator was asked why his speeches were so good, he replied, "Well, first I tells 'em what I'm goin' ta tell 'em; then I tells 'em; and then I tells 'em what I tole 'em."

A lack of preparation in making presentations is bad, and too much preparation is just as bad, because it may lead to too much information in too short a time period. Don't try and teach too much in one session. Do one or two ideas or skills well, and be pleased with that.

The most important aspect about delivery is to speak to your participants. As Florence Nelson warns, "You are not teaching skills or knowledge. You are teaching people. You must speak their language."[2] In speaking their language, you should be precise and economical in your words, speak clearly, and project your voice.

Try to reduce the numbers of "uhs" and "ers" you use, as well as any pet words or phrases that might become repetitious. The rest is pacing and timing; delicate and critical aspects of speaking best learned through practice.

Kenneth Eble, in his book *The Craft of Teaching,* has these do's and don'ts about making a good presentation.

Don't
- begin without an introduction,
- have a lack of contact with the audience,
- remain in a fixed position, with your attention on your notes, use a monotonous voice,
- display false modesty, use repeated hesitations,
- get into private quarrels with other authorities.

Do
- fit the material into the time allotted, seek precise examples and illustrations, stimulate the audience's interest,
- improvise,
- provide for breathing spaces and time for questions,
- provide an ending every time, but maintain a continuity with what lies ahead,
- develop a large range in voice, gestures and physical movement. Root out mannerisms and affectations. Listen to yourself,
- be guided by the audience.[3]

Steven Brookfield adds this important note: "One of the characteristics students value most in their teachers is authenticity. If you teach in a way that belies fundamental aspects of your personality, you will come across as stilted and inauthentic."[4]

Online Presentations

You can also record your presentations and put them in your online class-room. In fact, in formal education this is becoming a trend and will be very common in a few years.

There are at least two good reasons why you want to consider putting your presentations online:

1. Better use of class time. When your participants listen to your presentations and view your slides or visuals online, you can use your class time together for discussion, questions and answers, involving your participants, and helping them learn more individually and as a group.

2. Better learning of information. When your participants listen to your online presentations, they learn more. We each have a different part of the day or evening when we learn best, our "peak learning time." Online, your participants can listen to you when they are at their best. Online, you are always brilliant and at your best. If not, you simply delete it and start over. And online, you only create the presentation once and then you have more time to devote to helping your participants learn.

The easiest and most common way to do online presentations is to create a slideshow and then record to your slides. This is easy and inexpensive, usually no-cost. You can also record yourself as a video. Either way, chunk your presentations, keeping audio presentations to 10-20 minutes and video presentations around five minutes. You'll find you can say a lot online in a few minutes.

If you need technical help, it is worth the effort to find someone to help you, because your participants will benefit so much from your online presentations. For training on creating and delivering good online presentations, see *Advanced Teaching Online* or take one of our many online courses at TeachingOntheNet.org or UGotClass.net

Flipping the classroom. At the time of this writing, the term and practice of "flipping the classroom" is emerging. You should know about it, and for some of you, it might be relevant for your subject and your audience.

In a traditional formal education setting, usually the teacher delivers a lecture or presentation during class time, and then assigns homework or an assignment for after school. In the flipped classroom, students listen to the teacher online after school hours. And then they do their homework in class with the teacher better able to assist them with their work and learning.

It is an exciting and positive development in formal education, and it may have some relevance for your teaching as well.

How to Ask a Good Question

One of the more potent weapons in your teaching arsenal is the good question. With it, you can keep the group together, share values and ideas, and explore new horizons of possibilities. The good question can make your class exciting while the poor question can provoke boredom.

Many proper and beneficial uses for asking a question include:

- As a lubricant to keep the group together and interested.
- To argue or set up poles or opposites.
- To share exciting attitudes, values or ideas class members hold.
- To get participants to say things you would say but have greater effect when said by a participant.
- To explore deeper and come up with new ideas or understanding.
There are also poor uses of a question. Don't use a question to:
- To reprimand someone or test one's ignorance.
- To select or call attention to the better students.
- To fill time.
- To reach a forgone conclusion or lead people along a predetermined path.
- To put people on the spot; or when there is always a right and wrong answer to each of your questions.

Three types of questions. There are generally three types of questions. One is the question asking for facts or known information. These questions are good to open a discussion or presentation, to capture or rekindle the class's attention, to promote active listening, and of course, as recall or test questions. Some ways of phrasing the question include using some of these words: who, where, what, when, why, how, state, name, identify, list, describe, relate, tell, recall, give and locate.

There are questions of interpretation or evaluation. These questions ask people to compare, contrast, set a value on a certain item, or put something into perspective. They are useful in fostering critical thinking, and they are also good discussion questions. "Which alternative sources of energy show the most promise today?" is an example.

Some ways to phase an evaluative question include using one of these words: evaluate, analyze, judge, compare, contrast, differentiate, calculate, measure, appraise, deliberate, and estimate.

A third kind of question asks the participants to think deeper and come up with a creative answer usually not previously discussed. These questions urge people to think beyond what was known or talked about. "What would you

91

do if you could run the economy?" is one such question. Creative questions can start with any of these words: make, create, speculate, design, invent, construct, devise, predict, develop, what would have happened, and what would you have done.

Tips for asking good questions. Here are some tips on asking a good question.

- Ask questions that have few wrong answers and try to follow up incorrect answers with other questions that lead the class in the right direction without highlighting an incorrect statement.

- Follow up and answer with another question to the same person, or by asking the same question to another person, or by asking the follow-up question to another person. This generates ideas and builds the discussion level.

- To bring out different points of view or clarify missed points, ask a devil's advocate question that might not correlate to your own position but sheds more light on the topic.

- Diffuse the discussion among all the class members by asking a reaction question to those not involved in the discussion. "Maria, how do you feel about what Burt just said?" is one example.

- Silence after a question is not necessarily bad. Before trying another question or answering your own question, allow some silence to encourage thinking and participant responsibility for the discussion.

- Sometimes deliberately throwing questions to people on different sides of the room, or even going around the group with your questions helps build the level of involvement.

- If your participants start directing their answers and then their questions to each other, that can generate excellent participation and ideas.

You do not have to be the starting and ending point for each comment. You can encourage others to address each other with a nod or expression such as "Go ahead," indicating it is acceptable to address one another

Good questions to start a discussion are those asking for people's existing ideas, such as whether they agree or disagree about a particular issue. After letting them state present values or attitudes, you can then go on to more tough questions involving creative thinking or postulating.

When used in a class discussion, your questions should seek to stimulate discussion and involve as many people as possible. The discussion grows like a spiral, involving more people and rising to greater heights of ideas and thinking as you go. To help do that, think of questions that will fit together in a sequence or culminate in generating new ideas. As Kenneth Eble says, "My goal is to achieve a rhythm in a series of questions so the group arrives at moments of larger understanding."[5]

Arranging People

How you arrange the class often can determine the kind and extent of interaction you will have. Think carefully about how the seating arrangement will affect the discussion. For example, the more people can see each other, the more they will be involved in discussion. Thus, circles and U-shaped designs promote discussion. For more formal presentations and larger groups, banquet style seating is more appropriate. In banquet style, people sit at round tables and can discuss around the table.

Out-of-Class Experiences

In adult learning, the community can be your classroom. Resources abound in your community, and they can be tapped for a more stimulating and enriching course.

Here are some ideas:

- If guest speakers cannot come to you, go to them. Having them talk in their own workplace or surroundings will be more enjoyable, too.
- Have the class do investigative work in your local library.
- Go on a field trip in or out of town to a factory, work site, office, or company related to the subject you are studying.
- Visit a museum or local exhibition.
- Attend a meeting of a citizens' group, community action group, club, or organization working with the problem you are discussing.
- Conduct a class or two in a non-class setting, such as a park, restaurant, or tavern, as a way of stimulating a different and more open kind of discussion.
- Take advantage of conventions, conferences, and other gatherings happening in your area during the time of your session.
- Send class members out to interview media people, business leaders,

workers, ministers, or other people associated with the topic you are studying.

Small Group Activities

Using intra-group activities can enhance your teaching in many ways. The activities will give your participants a different perspective on the topic, allowing them to act in different roles and engage in discussion. Interaction with other participants leads to greater learning and provides creative breaks to stimulate your students.

There are countless ways to involve your participants, each with a slightly different twist and each one appropriate to a certain kind of topic or learning environment. Experiment with one or more even if you have never tried or even heard of them before.

In designing the experiences, mentally preview them yourself beforehand to simulate what might occur and what you need to set them up. Most of these exercises cannot be completed in 10 or 15 minutes. Allow time to divide into groups, introduce the concept and develop it, have closure, and time to become a class again.

Here are some common and uncommon ways to enhance your class:

Brainstorming. As a class, or in groups, people try to generate a wide variety of ideas, suggestions, and possibilities. In brainstorming, one is not allowed to criticize or evaluate an idea or suggestion. Usually all of the ideas are written down and later distilled, compared, or used by the entire group. The object is to fantasize, break down barriers, and elicit a variety of ideas from every person in the group.

Role playing. Two or more class members act out a real or hypothetical situation, usually taking roles not normally associated with that person. The object is to see the situation from another's perspective.

Case incidents. Analyzing a real-life situation or case incident, different class members assume different positions on the issue in raising pros and cons.

Committee. The class breaks into or forms a committee to decide policy, study, or formulate ideas on a given topic. A position paper or list of recommendations may be the outcome.

Sensitivity group. Members of the group engage in various sensitivity exercises designed to bring out feelings and share experiences with each other in a new way. For types of sensitivity exercises, see Sense Relaxation: Below Your Mind by Bernard Gunther, New York: Collier Books, 1968.

Task force. The group engages in a specific mission trying to accomplish a given task. The task force then reports back to the rest of the class on progress and achievement.

Panel. Class members are chosen to engage in a discussion in front of the rest of the class, usually with one person serving as moderator. The panel format brings out different viewpoints and encourages discussion without taking sides.

Debate. Unlike a panel, a debate is designed to take sides and bring out opposite viewpoints. Usually with teams of two to four members each, participants present and then argue the pros and cons. A vote can be taken to choose the winning team if desired.

Interview. One or two members of the class can invite a guest speaker to be interviewed. Usually the interviewers prepare specific questions for the speaker to answer, and sometimes questions are taken from the class as well. This is a good way to use outside resources without listening to a speech.

Listening team. Divide the class into groups of three: a speaker, a listener, and an observer. One person relates his or her experiences or ideas on the topic to another person, with the listening person questioning, repeating, and restating key phrases for clarification. The third person observes the entire process, and after a time limit, reports to the other two on what he observed. The people then shift roles and repeat so each person has a chance to be a speaker, listener, and observer.

Network group. The network group is made up of class members who meet together from time to time, either scheduled or not, to talk about a specific topic or simply to share problems.

Reaction panel. A small number of class members react to a talk, film, or other presentation with their observations. The goal is to get a critical review and class input.

Chapter 11.
Energizing the Learning Environment

"Some 25 percent of learning depends
on the physical environment."

— U.S. Department of Education study

The last letter of DIVE —E —stands for Energizing the learning environment. Here we focus on an area with enormous potential to enhance your session and improve your participants' learning — the physical learning environment.

The physical learning environment is composed of four elements:

1. The learning room, the human-built environment in which your session takes place;

2. Teaching tools, those physical objects that help convey your message;

3. The natural environment, such as temperature and time of day;

4. Learning mediums, those physical objects that set the stage, reduce barriers, act as stimulators, and assist your participants to learn.[1]

We can chart the four elements in this way:

WORLD		POSITION	
		EXTERNAL	INTERNAL
	HUMAN-BUILT	The Learning Room	Teaching Tools
	NATURAL	Natural Environment	Learning Mediums

97

Our response as presenters and teachers to the physical environment needs to be a departure from most of our previous experience. Instead of passive acceptance and inaction with regard to the physical environment, we can change our response to the physical environment. We can move to actively engaging the physical environment.

We can adjust our teaching to accommodate it, in the case of the natural environment; modify it, in the case of the room and room setup; improve it, in the case of our teaching tools; or most actively, create it, in the case with learning mediums.

In the next four sections, we look at each of these components of the physical learning environment and how you can take advantage of them to enhance your teaching and presenting.

The Learning Room

The learning room where your session meets may be called many things: conference room, ballroom, boardroom, or even class room, but never a learning room. Although your meeting room has been carefully designed and constructed, rarely is a room engineered to reflect how adults learn.

Most built environments are intended for purposes other than learning. Compounding the structural inadequacy of most meeting rooms are two problems of perhaps greater detriment to your participants' learning success. The first is that most of us as presenters do not understand the impact of the physical environment on our session's success, and the second is that most of us as presenters don't know what to do about it. Consequently, most meeting rooms are left untouched by the presenter or instructor, even down to the location of the chairs. The fact of the physical environment of too many educational sessions is thus left in the hands of the building's custodial staff.

Only a few of us may have the chance to build a physical learning space for our sessions. Yet all of us could modify the existing physical space to enhance our participants' learning and their satisfaction with our performance.

You can modify your meeting room in many ways, and the building's custodial staff is often more than willing to help. Before your session begins, you have an opportunity to improve upon its success by the way you modify the room arrangements.

One of the more critical decisions you will make for any session is how to set up the room. There are different ways to set up a room, each with different characteristics to it, each giving the participants a different sense of what is to happen and how they can be involved. The right room setup can contribute greatly to create the kind of situation and interaction you want in your class or session.

The room setup will determine:

• Visibility and ability to hear.

• The formality or informality of the session.

• The level to which you want the participants to be involved in discussion.

• The relationship between you as instructor or presenter and your participants.

• The group dynamics that will take place.

Room setup is one of the more critical ways you construct the kind of learning environment for your class or session.

The most common styles of room setup are these six:

1. Theater

2. Classroom

3. U-shape

4. Conference or square

5. Banquet

6. Chairs in a circle.

The *theater* style room setup has traditionally been used for speeches, lectures, and more formal one-way communication. To enhance interaction, move yourself closer to your participants, encourage them to sit closer to the front, adjust the seating to center around you, and knock down, as best you can, the formal podium speaker setup.

Classroom-style is an instructional mode, theater style with tables or desks added for note-taking ease.

The *U-shape* setup has interaction and participation built in.

Banquet-style has some of the large capacity qualities of theater style but with small group interaction possibilities.

Conference-style seating is a more formal setting for small groups.

Circle-style seating maximizes participation and discussion, with the teacher often acting more as a facilitator and moderator than a presenter. Circle seating is not used often enough, perhaps because some presenters and teachers are needlessly defensive or threatened by its lack of hierarchy, its openness, and its invitation to total participant involvement. Whatever the case, circle style seating should be used in more educational sessions.

Teaching Tools

Teaching tools are those physical objects that enhance your teaching and improve your participants' learning. They are enormously powerful tools and we have generally only scratched the surface of their potential.

Few presenters and teachers use their teaching tools effectively. Most misunderstand and misuse them. Most people call teaching tools "audio-visual aids" or AV for short. AV is a limiting term. Here we will expand beyond audio-visual aids to include all physical aids in teaching.

Keys to Great Slides

At the time of this writing, slide presentations represent one of the most widely used, and misused, ways of communicating with your audience.

Slide presentations represent an enormously varied tool for you to communicate visually with your participants. At the time of this writing, PowerPoint has been joined by Prezi and SlideRocket as slide presentation software options.

Slides add to your teaching for at least two reasons. One is that people learn visually, and visual complements to your words increase learning. The second is that people listen faster than you can speak, and so your slides provide additional visual information.

Nevertheless, slides are also one of the great misused communication tools. Too many presenters simply talk to the slides. You should not be merely reading the words on the slides. If you are doing this, the slides have become a script instead of a visual communication, and you have lost the visual capability to help you teach.

Here are the keys to great slides:

Make slides visual. Most presenters err by putting only words on their slides. Visual communication takes place with images - pictures, photos, artwork, clip art, and drawings.

Use few words. If you want to put your learners to sleep, use lots of words. Instead, put as few words on your slides as possible. Your slides are not a script for you to read. And put words in large enough type size to make them visible from the back of the room. The minimum size is 28 point.

Use more color. Use color as background. Use colored boxes. Put some words in color. Color stimulates the eye and the brain.

Don't have too many. It is better to have a few good slides than too many. If you are racing through the slides at the end of your presentation, you have too many slides.

Make them visual. To make your slides visual,

• Convey only one concept per slide.

• Use only a few words. Eliminate unnecessary words.

• Think of a picture that illustrates what you are trying to say.

• There are pictures that directly relate to content. And then there are pictures that suggest the content. For example, if you are cautioning people not to be narrow-minded, a picture of an ostrich might be a good suggestive picture.

• With some exceptions, one picture is better than multiple pictures.

• Make the picture as large as you can. The visual should take up as much of the slide screen as possible. The most effective visuals dominate the screen.

• Ask if the words relate to the picture. The words should be tied to the picture when viewed. If you have one whole, with the words and picture making sense together, you have a good visual slide.

Using sound and motion. If you are already using good visuals for your slides, think about taking your slide show to a more advanced level. Make it a more multimedia experience by incorporating sound and/or motion. This is also how you can do online presentations, using the technology already available in your slide show software, or any number of software supplements.

Using audio. Audio files can be embedded to play automatically when a given slide is shown. Three kinds of audio that are effective in the teaching situation include:

• Sound effects. Short sounds, like applause, a waterfall, etc., that last for only a few seconds.

- Quotes and speech excerpts. Words from another speaker, such as from a famous speech, a quote, a poem, or a news broadcast.
- Music. The fair-use guidelines indicate that teachers can use up to 29 seconds of a song without requiring either permission or payment.

Motion. There are several ways to incorporate motion into your slides.

- Words, colored bars, and pictures can "fly" into a slide.
- Slides can rotate quickly to create a sense of motion.
- Video can be embedded in a slide so that you can show a clip from a movie, television show, or home movie.
- Use audio and sound sparingly. Just one audio or video clip can make a big impression. Too many dilute the impact and your message.

Set up instructions

In delivering your slide presentation, take into consideration the following:

1. Where you stand. Plan ahead where you will stand so that your participants can see the screen. You also do not want to stand too far away from your participants and become distant from them.

2. Set up ahead of time. Set up your slide show ahead of time. Waste as little time in the class as possible rearranging audio-visuals. Every second in class is precious, and even taking a minute may reduce the enthusiasm or readiness to learn.

3. Adjust the lighting. The ideal is to have the screen slightly darkened, with the participant seating area in plenty of light. Unfortunately, almost all rooms do not have lighting designs suitable for slide presentations. Nevertheless it is worth fiddling with the lights to get the best possible lighting.

Devices and Aids

Devices and aids help you present the material in an interesting, clear or different manner. They make your presentation more interesting. Here are just some of the tools that can help your teaching.

Flip chart. Sometimes called the "adult blackboard," the flip chart is visually pleasing and enables you to function more spontaneously than relying only on prepared slides. Use a large or jumbo-sized marker. Black and blue are the best colors for copy. Use red and green for highlighting.

Audio and music. Good for drama, speeches, and to illustrate with music, whether tapes, CDs, downloads or other audio formats. For quotes and speeches, hearing the original often has more of an effect on listeners.

Video. Video is a powerful tool if used as a supplement to your presentation. The most stimulating uses of video are as short segments to illustrate your presentation. Severely limit your video segments to no more than 10 percent of your total meeting time. Most video segments should last no more then ten minutes.

Charts and graphs. Good for illustrating data, statistics, figures and comparisons. In fact, we understand data better when conveyed by charts and graphs than by text.

Props. There's nothing like a good prop to gain interest and make a point. From clothing items to tools or accessories, props almost always light up eyes and gain greater attention and retention.

Magic kit. Use the Magic _____ Kit (you fill in the blank) to high-light important points. Find some toys or other make-believe or fantasy items to illustrate each point. Wrap a box in colored paper and your kit is complete.

Puppets. There are some things that a puppet can say that you as the teacher cannot.

Magazines, books, articles. You can talk about an article. Or you can bring it in and show it. The latter technique, used sparingly and for just a minute or so, is another effective teaching aid.

Posters and pictures. Posters and pictures on the walls liven up the whole learning environment. When your learners get up and stand in front of them, you also have incorporated movement into the learning, enhancing the retention effect.

Web shots and web sites. Going live on the Internet can be an effective way to illustrate a point or explore unusual resources, such as animations and simulations. It's best to have the web site already up when you're reading to talk about it, so doing it first or after a break is a good time. Time spent in navigating the web may lead to boredom or disinterest, so considering incorporating still web shots into your PowerPoint slides rather than going live online.

Mobiles and computers in class. At the time of this writing, there is emerging the practice of using cell phones or mobiles in the classroom. Integrating the resources of the web into the face-to-face classroom is an exciting new development. People learn by doing, and younger adults are especially attuned to using computers for learning. Computers offer interactivity and individualization, both positive contributions to learning. Mobiles are one more tool for you the teacher. Find the mobile strategy that is appropriate for your class. It may be going online during a presentation, responding to questions, accessing your online classroom, or a group activity. Generally, a computer-related activity should be limited to a portion of the class time, such as 20 minutes, for maximum attention and retention.

Reading Lists, Handouts, and Exercises

Readings. There are many stories of the teacher who shows up for the first class of a 10-session course with a list of 10 books for the class to read. With a full work day and other obligations, most adults would be lucky to read one book in ten weeks. Yet literature has been a big part of learning for most of us, and we want to convey the classics in our field, or have participants do some reading.

For many classes, outside reading may be completely unnecessary. For other classes, you may be able to convey ideas and concepts through audio-visual methods rather than the print medium.

Where outside reading is advantageous, you can make it easier for your students to do the reading by:

1. Limiting the reading list to one book, preferably a paperback.
2. Recommending chapters of a book, or copying chapters of a book, following the copyright laws, for your students.
3. Finding appropriate pamphlets and booklets.
4. Using articles from magazines.
5. Constructing your own summaries of longer works.

Handouts. Generally, learners love handouts. They are perceived as an extra benefit. But you should select carefully the type and number of handouts.

Use these tips in providing handouts:
• Spread them out. It is better to have one or two per meeting rather than having some meetings with lots of handouts and others with none.

- Distribute them separately. Handouts will be valued more and given more attention when you hand them out separately rather than providing the handouts all at once.

- Colored paper is awesome. Colored paper really generates attention. Different colors of paper also distinguish one hand out from another. Put the handout with the most pages on white stock. Put others with lots of copy on light colored stock. Save dark colored paper for handouts with little copy, large copy, or charts.

- Design them attractively. Some handouts have to be words all over the page, but other handouts should be simply yet attractively designed with white space, bulleted points, headlines, and some italicized or boldfaced type.

Exercises. Exercise papers and worksheets engage your participants in the learning process and keep them physically active and alert in class. They also are a non-judgmental way of instructing and testing because the participant is not competing with anyone else.

Paper exercises help people learn, and they break up the class and make it more interesting. Some kinds of paper exercises are worksheets, puzzles, crossword puzzles, quizzes, illustrations, and problem-solving exercises.

Ebooks and online resources. Ebooks and online resources are another way to deliver information to your learners. Yet some research shows that even younger learners often prefer hard copy text to electronic sources, so choose the format or combination that you think is best. With handouts, we do know that physical hard copy handouts are very effective for all learners, even if other resources are electronic.

The Natural Environment

Although most learning situations take place indoors in human built buildings, we cannot escape our natural environment and its effect on our learning and teaching.

Lighting

"Lights up" is the word for illuminating your learning room. Too much artificial light is rarely a problem, but there are thousands of cases in which too little artificial light is a problem.

If you are meeting in a room that has too little light, try hard to do something about it. Find out if someone can turn up the lights. Bring in a couple of standing lamps from home if you need to. Ask about getting the room switched. Open the shades if there are windows and your meeting is during the day.

Sunlight or natural light can be a problem. Glare, looking into the sun, and the sun's rays can all make it more difficult to see. The sun's rays change during the course of your session. For all these reasons, monitor the sunlight in your room carefully throughout your session. If that is a hassle, close the blinds if there is enough artificial light in the room. A little sunlight perks people up, but too much can be a big distraction.

Noise

Nothing destroys a good session like outside noise. Take what ever precautionary measures you can to prevent outside noise from interfering. If it happens, seek to diminish the effect.

If you are in a room with permanent walls, you are in good shape. But if there are partitions for walls, such as in a ballroom or hotel, check out the partitions. If the partitions are solid, you are in fairly good shape. Solid partitions are one inch or so thick and have more sound resistance. If the partition is a single piece of material and is siding, then you may have a noise problem.

Temperature

The physical comfort of the room is a factor in how well we are able to listen, interact, and stay focused.

The basic rule in gauging whether your participants are too hot or too cold is that your opinion does not count. As the instructor or presenter, you may be standing up, have more air space around you than your participants, may be at a different end of the room, and you are absorbed in your presentation and facilitating the discussion. Unfortunately, your participants are less absorbed, and temperature affects them.

The best advice I have heard has come from seminar guru Anver Suleiman. He urges that participants be given a list of suggestions before the educational meeting or program starts, perhaps with a confirmation statement. One of the suggestions that always would be included is to encourage each participant to wear "layered clothing." This means wear or bring a sweater, jacket, suit coat, or sweater vest. Then if the participants are too hot, they can shed some clothing; and if the room is too cool, they can keep the sweater on. In this way, you as instructor or presenter shift the responsibility for proper temperature control to your participants. You may still have to deal with any failures or excesses in heating or cooling equipment, but you have restricted your responsibility and encouraged your participants to anticipate the situation.

Learning Mediums

Learning mediums differ from teaching tools. Learning mediums are physical objects which set the stage, reduce barriers, act as stimulators, or otherwise enhance the physical learning environment. Learning mediums occupy a middle ground between the presenter and participant. They often surround or envelop the participant. Sometimes they are the substance through which an effect is transmitted.

View the learning mediums offered here as choices and alternatives. Use them as you see fit, as often or as sparingly as appropriate for your learning situations. They are not advocated with equal intensity or as a group.

Playing music before your session starts helps to get your participants into a learning mode in at least two ways.

First, music breaks the awkward silence.

Second, some kinds of music actually can help put people into a learning mode. The Lind Institute in San Francisco, for example, has tapes of classical music constructed with a certain number of beats per minute. This timing is supposed to be the same as our internal "clock" and helps put participants into a learning mode.[2]

Flowers have a calming, engaging, and spritely effect on a group. They are an excellent visual aid in creating a good learning environment.

Presents for your participants are an unexpected pleasure. Few participants come to an educational session expecting to receive a gift. Competition for presents not only immediately gears up an audience, but also subtly lets them know the topic being addressed is important. And presents give you a great opportunity for humor.

Ribbons are special. I used to think ribbons were just for important people and leaders of educational events. In the last few years, my thinking has changed entirely. I think everyone should have a ribbon.

Aroma impacts the learning environment, with positive smells subtly encouraging learning and negative smells having a detrimental effect. Some positive aroma tips include: bake a pie; put vanilla on a light bulb; use a potpourri; burn incense; heat a pot of coffee; or neutralize the air with an air freshener.

Mints and hard candy. Mints or hard candy are a welcome treat. Often they are well received after a break.

Food and drink can facilitate and boost learning. And when meals are too heavy, food can be a detriment to learning.

A little bit of food and drink can go a long way to create a positive learning environment, generate group cohesiveness, and create participant involvement and satisfaction.

What we have tried to do in this chapter is to explore the concept that the physical environment and physical objects do affect learning. One can reduce barriers, stimulate learners' interest, create a learning atmosphere, and complement one's instruction or presentation by using a variety of physical factors.

Part III.
Improving Your Teaching

Chapter 12.
Measuring Results

*"Changingness, a reliance on process rather than
upon static knowledge, is the only thing that makes
any sense as a goal for education."*

— Carl R. Rogers, renowned social psychologist

In some learning situations, it is either difficult or not particularly relevant for learners to assess and measure what they have gained from a course. In other learning situations, however, it is either important or necessary to measure participants' progress.

There are several new and positive developments regarding assessment in the learning situation:

1. Assessment improves learning. Recent research now shows that measuring one's learning actually improves learning. And the more frequently a learner's progress is measured, the more assessment aids in the learning. So evaluating someone's learning no longer is an end-of-course measurement, and no longer something limited to the formal education setting.

2. Learners want completion records. Many if not most learners now have a desire to document their learning and show they have completed your course or curriculum. You can see the increase in certificates, certifications, badges, continuing education units, and other records. This feeling of completion also engenders a positive internal satisfaction on the part of the learner, all of which is good.

3. Online assessment available. Online classrooms now have built-in

113

quiz functions that make frequent self-testing easy and helpful.

So we are going to assume here that it is likely that some assessment will be relevant to your subject matter and audience.

Defining Terminal Goals

When planning courses in which measuring student progress is important, Verduin, in *Adults Teaching Adults,* recommends that you first define your terminal goals and then assess entering behavior or knowledge before assessing learning.[1]

Defining terminal goals for the learner should be stated in terms of either knowledge skills, or behavioral objectives.

Knowledge skills

For many, if not most classes for adults, acquiring knowledge is the goal. Try these suggestions in designing knowledge objectives:

- Use the adult student as the subject of the objective. For example: "The learner will know ..."
- State specifically what the student is expected to know as a result of the learning.
- Specify how the knowledge is to be demonstrated so that learning can be assessed.
- Write your knowledge objectives in complete sentences.

Behavioral objectives

For skills-based, workplace, and occupational courses, behavioral objectives may be more appropriate. In his book *"Objectives to Outcomes: Your Contract with the Learner,"* Glen Ramsborg suggests the ABC approach to writing instructional objectives.

- **Audience.** At the conclusion of this lecture, the attendee/learner will be able to: _. It is important to think of this statement when constructing an objective. It defines your audience and can be placed only at the beginning of the listing of the outcomes for a specific learning event.
- **Behavior or knowledge skill.** The desired knowledge skill is indicated by the action verb. It is the "what" of the learner's contract with the teacher. It tells the learner how the information can be used after

the learning situation has taken place.

• **Condition.** Conditions are the situational variables that are written specifically for the program and are, in essence, the program content.

Ramsborg goes on to say, "The most important characteristic of a useful objective is that it describes the kind of performance that will be accepted as evidence that the learner has mastered the outcome."

From designing knowledge objectives or outcomes desired at the end of the course, you can move to writing instructional objectives or those objectives to be achieved during the class, as opposed to knowledge objectives, which are to be achieved after the course ends.

Instructional objectives should be brief enough to be remembered, clear enough to be written, and specific enough to be obtainable.[2]

Management specialist Robert Mager offers these hints on instructional objectives.

An instructional objective:

1. Says something about the learner.

2. Identifies an observable act - what the learner will be able to do.

3. Is about ends rather than means.

4. Describes conditions under which the learner will be performing the behavior.

5. Contains information about the level of performance that will be considered acceptable.[3]

Assessing Entering Knowledge

Assessing the knowledge of your participants before they take your course or program is an exciting if emerging process that almost certainly will become standard for all kinds of learning situations in the future. With the availability of online quizzes, pre-assessment becomes easy and quick. Pre-assessment helps determine what the person has learned during the course. It helps you understand what areas of the course to stress, and of which areas your participants may already be familiar.

To do a pre-assessment:

• For hands-on skills, have the student attempt to perform the desired task or series of skills; or

- Measure your incoming learner's knowledge with a quiz, such as an online quiz. A simple ten question quiz, with questions at three levels of complexity-basic, moderate, and advanced-will give you a good idea what each of your incoming participants knows, and does not know, already.

Assessing Learning

Assessing an adult's learning properly can help him or her immensely. Good assessment is not merely testing outcomes; it also helps an adult learn. By providing an accurate picture of what a student knows or can do, it provides that person with:

- Satisfaction in one's achievements.
- Encouragement to learn more.
- Direction in what knowledge areas still need to be acquired. By assessing your students' learning, you also gain by understanding how to improve your course, such as what areas need more emphasis and what areas are sufficiently covered for most students.

Midway tests

By conducting one or more tests during the course, both student and teacher gain valuable information about where the student is, and what needs to be done during the rest of the course.

These tests can be short and still be effective. They need not take a lot of your time. Consider multiple choice and short answer tests.

You can also utilize other students in the course to help evaluate tests given during the course. When other students participate in the evaluation, the peer review helps them learn more as well.

Ungraded self-quizzes

One assessment and learning tool being used by more teachers is the ungraded self-quiz. With a self-quiz, often a multiple choice or short answer quiz of four to 10 questions, the quiz does not count towards any final grade or score.

The answers are graded immediately and returned to the student for immediate feedback. Many ungraded self-quizzes are thus done online so a computer can instantly grade and return the quiz scores to the student. The immediacy of the feedback is important to learners.

As the teacher, you then can see where your students are proficient and where additional work needs to be done.

Ungraded self-quizzes are heartily recommended as a win-win for both learners and teacher.

We test differently.

If we as students do not all learn in the same way, it follows that we test differently as well. Be aware that one kind of test or assessment may not accurately gauge the knowledge or skills learned by all of your students.

For example, one time a teacher asked students to read a book. To make sure each student had read the book, the teacher gave a test on it. One student couldn't answer any questions on the test, such as "who was the hero of the story?" When interviewed by the teacher, however, the student gave such complete and detailed responses, including why a variety of characters in the story could lay legitimate claim to being the hero, that it was obvious this student had indeed read the entire book.

So too, you need to be alert to the possibility that one or more of your students may require an alternative method of assessment.

Multiple assessments

More and more teachers are using several different assessments throughout the duration of the course. This is partly because we each test differently, and partly because it is difficult for one test to assess all aspects of one's learning.

Some teachers are including class discussion as one of the assessments, especially when online discussion is taking place as part of the course. Others are complementing tests with projects, presentations and other assessments which demonstrate knowledge. Still other teachers are incorporating group assessments, even to the extent of having students in the group evaluate each other's performance in the group activity.

There is clearly a direction towards teachers employing a variety of assessments.

Kinds of Assessments

Teachers are creating an increasing array of assessments. Here are some of them:

- **Essays.** Students write on a selected or their choice of theme.
- **Personal journal.** The student writes his or own reflections, including his or her thought process.
- **Role playing.** An individual assumes the role of a real or imagined person.
- **Debate.** Singly or in teams, your students argue different sides of an issue.
- **Learner presentations.** Individuals present ideas, information or research.
- **Group presentations.** Teams work together on a presentation.
- **Individual projects.** From a physical construction to community activity, project ideas are profuse.
- **Group projects.** Sometimes students evaluate each other at the end of the project.
- **Skill-based performance.** Often a practitioner can help evaluate the task.
- **Jeopardy or other games.** Turning tests into games can increase the learning.
- **Interviews.** You can interview a student.
- **Verbal tests.** Especially relevant for those students who have better verbal than written skills.
- **Slide shows.** Students can present information more visually.
- **Self assessments.** Teachers having students evaluate themselves report surprising self-awareness and positive results.

Decline of Time-Based Assessment

In the last century, time input was equated with learning for many adults. That is, if one sat in a class for a given length of time, one was judged to have learned a specified amount of knowledge. A common standard for adults has been 10 hours of seat time, equivalent to one continuing education unit, or CEU.

Equating seat time with learning is declining as an assessment standard for adult learning.

Separate behavior from knowledge

In assessing your students' learning, it is now important to separate unrelated behavior from knowledge acquisition. It is best to assess knowledge gained and not to confuse behavior with learning. Think twice about including such unrelated behavior as attendance, turning in an assignment late, dress, politeness, arguing with the teacher, handwriting, manuscript submission guidelines and neatness.

Including behavior as part of a grade distorts and misrepresents what really is or is not learned. It often has the painful side effect of discouraging or even alienating a learner.

Grading versus an objective standard

One of the trends in assessment is that we are moving away from assessing a student by comparing him or her with other students, and moving towards assessment that compares the learner to an objective standard. This is a concern particularly for adults, especially in the workplace, where employers and workers are increasingly benchmarking their skills and knowledge to an objective standard.

If you want your students to be ranked in relation to the other members in the class, you would use a typical grading system such as A, B, C, D and F, with the average grade supposedly being a C.

Although such comparative grading is common in formal schooling, be sure that ranking an individual in terms of others is helpful before awarding this kind of assessment. A graduating class of airplane pilots illustrates the increasing relevance of objective standards. You may have had someone tell you, "Did you know that 50 percent of the pilots today graduated in the bottom half of their class?" Although this is true, each graduating pilot was also judged by an objective standard that ensured that each pilot was fully qualified to fly an airplane

An objective standard sets a benchmark which any and all students can and should achieve. The benchmark is an endorsed quality standard that does not change much over time. The goal is for as many individuals to achieve the standard as possible.

119

One such objective standard being employed for a variety of adult learning experiences is the International Learning Unit, or outcome-based evaluation composed of five content items learned, with a pass rate of 80 percent (© LERN). A common evaluation is a test, and a comment content item is a question, so passing a quiz of five questions by getting four correct answers would gain 0.1 ILU. Other types of evaluations include demonstrations, essays, online discussion, presentations and other outcomes-based evaluations. If you are interested in learning more about the ILU, visit **www.LearningUnit.org.**

Guidelines for Constructing Tests

Tests are still prevalent in adult learning courses.

The British educator H.R. Mills warns that a test should be comprehensive, noting, "We all know the feeling of being unfairly treated when confronted by an examination paper that tests only a small fraction of what we have been working hard at, and encouraged to prepare."[4]

Following up with your participants on the results of their tests is helpful. Kenneth Eble says, "Giving feedback on an examination is as necessary and as worthy of care, intelligence, and imagination as making the test in the first place."[5]

The following are some guidelines for multiple choice tests and essay exams.[6]

Multiple Choice Items

1. Each item should test one, and only one, central idea.
2. Each item should be independent of every other item. One item should not aid in answering another item.
3. Avoid textbook phraseology and examples; whenever feasible, use new situations and terms.
4. The item stem should present the central problem and all qualifications; it should include all words that otherwise would occur in each alternative.
5. Avoid negatively stated items whose wording is confusing.
6. Alternatives should be homogenous in content, form, and grammatical structure.

7. There should be one, and only one, correct answer; this alternative should be clearly incorrect.

8. All distracters should be plausible and attractive to students who do not know the correct answer; yet they should be clearly incorrect or inadequate.

9. Alternatives should not overlap, include, or be synonymous with each other.

Essay Questions

1. The question should clearly and unambiguously define the task for the student, but without interfering with the measurement of the intended outcome.

2. The question should indicate the direction and scope of answer desired.

3. The question should require the student to demonstrate his command of essential background knowledge.

4. Use questions that have clearly acceptable answers rather than ones that measure only opinions or attitudes.

5. It is usually better to use more specific questions that can be answered briefly, rather than fewer broad, general questions.

6. Do not use optional questions.

7. Start essay questions with phrases such as "Compare and contrast," "Present the arguments for and against," "Give the reasons for," "Explain how (or why)," "Give an example of," and similar phrases.[7]

Chapter 13.
Improving Your Course

"Most of the shadows in this life are caused
by standing in one's own sunshine."

— Unkown

"I'm an excellent teacher. I'm the best," she said. She said it, her students said it, former students said it, and the schools where she taught said it. But something was wrong.

Elaine Norona was a professional dancer, and a professional dance instructor. She had trained at the Arthur Murray studios. She had spent ten years in the Far East as a professional belly dancer, and when she returned to Denver, she began teaching professionally at several different schools. "I can teach anything," she said. And it was true. One time a couple needed to know how to dance a minuet. Elaine had seen it performed one time on a late night television movie, and taught it to them. But there was something wrong with her class in dance.

It wasn't her first class. She had taught scores, maybe hundreds of scores, of classes before. But the students were restless. They were complaining. And she was uncomfortable, too. She began to talk about her students, how they didn't respect her, didn't dress for class very well, didn't look right.

So the school administrator, Tracy Dunning, decided to find out what was wrong with the class and to make it better. After talking to both Elaine and the students, she discovered that Elaine had certain expectations of her students, and in particular, their appearance and dress. Some chewed gum.

The women did not wear dresses. And the students unconsciously felt Elaine's unhappiness, and so they became restless and unhappy as well.

Tracy solved the problem by having Elaine write down her expectations of the students: no gum chewing, proper dress, and so on. And before the next class, Elaine went over her expectations with the students. Fortunately, she explained to them humorously rather than citing them as rules, and so the students then knew what to expect and could act accordingly.

Most classes do not get that kind of attention and help, and thus, too many classes are not improved when they could be. But Elaine recognized not only that good teachers need help every once in a while, but also that evaluation can be non-threatening and can improve one's class. And Tracy Dunning was a good administrator, recognizing that most problems in classes for adults can be solved. By asking the students to help and by working to solve the problem, together they made it a better class.

All teachers, even the best ones, can improve their teaching. You can revise your class and do it in a way that says you are a good teacher.

Fail Early, Fail Often

That bit of advice comes from a number of sources and wise teachers.

You, like every other teacher, are a pioneer when it comes to teaching adults. There is no one way to success. And the learning and teaching environment keeps changing.

Fail early. Don't wait to try a new idea. Instead try a new technique or idea early. If you fail early, you will be able to correct it by the time it really matters.

Fail often. For every course, try one or two new things. Try not to try lots of new things all at once, as you will not be able to distinguish what worked from what did not work. If you are trying something new each course, you will always look forward to the next course.

How to Improve Your Course

Every time you offer your course, or any course, evaluate it and make improvements in your teaching for the next time.[1]

The best time to improve your course is during or immediately after you teach it. Do not wait until you offer it the next time to make improvements.

124

You will have lost the edge, both cognitively and energy-wise, in tackling the essence of the improvements.

There are three important items to know to improve your course.

1. **What learners really like.** This is actually more important to know than what they want to see changed. The positive aspects, the winning techniques, the great stuff- is what makes your course a success. You have to know what works, so you can keep it and do it again.

2. **What learners want to see changed.** You need to evaluate whether only one or two participants want to see something changed or whether the comments reflect a significant enough portion of the class participants that you should attempt a change.

3. **Prioritize your changes.** Select the one to three items to change for your next course. You don't need to change everything. You don't want to change more than a few high priority aspects of your course.

Use this chart to help you decide what one to three items to change for your next course.

	TAKES MORE TIME	TAKES LESS TIME
VERY IMPORTANT	Work on over several course offerings	Best items to change
LESS IMPORTANT	Avoid changes here	Only if they can be done quickly and painlessly

Write it down. If you can jot down your one to three priorities for changing your course in your files, on a notepad or in a computer file, you will greatly increase your chances of actually accomplishing those changes and improving your course.

How to Do an Evaluation

An evaluation should be simple and as short as possible. Here is the best evaluation ever designed. It has been tested with thousands of learners over many years. It is superior to any other standard evaluation.

The evaluation has two questions:

1."Overall, were you satisfied with the course? ____yes ___no"
2."(Optional) Comments or testimonial:" (space or three to five lines for copy is provided.

Here's why it is the best evaluation:

High response. There is actually only one question, and what we know is that the fewer the questions asked, the higher the response rate. So more of your participants are likely to respond to this evaluation than any other evaluation.

One clear question. The question, "Overall, were you satisfied with the course?" is clear and unambiguous. There is little room for interpretation or misunderstanding.

From looking at hundreds of other evaluations, we also know that "course" and "teacher" are synonymous in the minds of learners. There is no distinction. So there is no need to ask an additional question about you the teacher.

The yes/no response categories are also simple and unambiguous. If you receive any responses that say "no" then you know the person was dissatisfied and you would want to follow up with that person.

The yes/no response categories are also superior to the Likert scale, the 1 to 5 rating. For one thing, what is one participant's '3' might be another participant's '4.' And in a typical class the overall Likert score will likely be 3.8 or 3.6, and these numbers just do not give you much information about what to do, or not do, better.

The yes/no categories also give you as the teacher a great publicity number, the percentage of people who say they were satisfied with your course. Typically that percentage will be very high, very positive, and you can use that number both in promoting your course, and in verifying to organizations and entities your worth as a teacher.

A second, open ended, optional questions requesting "Comments or testimonial" is also the best question to solicit more information.

For one, it is optional and learners who do not have anything else to tell you will still turn in the evaluation. So again, it helps create a high response rate, which is very important.

It tells you what they liked. Second, the question means you will get some comments about what the participant liked, the positive aspects of your course. This information is actually more important than what participants want to see changed. You as the teacher really need to pay attention to what people liked about your class, because those aspects are your strengths, things you want to continue, things that might encourage future participants to take your course.

Better than a laundry list. A single open ended question is better than a laundry list of questions for two reasons. First, the more questions you have the lower the response rate and thus the lower the validity of the data. Second, the laundry list of questions inevitably leaves out something that one or more of your participants thinks is important, so you miss valuable input from your students. With the open ended question, you almost always get information that is deemed important to the participant and information the person wants you to know. So you can easily see what is important to the learner.

Best tool for testimonials. Testimonials are golden. They are the best marketing tool for your course ever invented. With this simple evaluation form, you will also get several testimonials that you can use in many ways for your future offerings.

All in all, this evaluation is easy to distribute, either in-person or online, easy to complete, easy to tally, and most of all you get comments and information that your participants think is important and valuable.

Best time. The best time to ask your participants for their evaluations is just before, or during the last class meeting. After the course is over is too late, people will have forgotten already what they might have suggested and will be thinking about their next activity, not their last one.

Mid-course evaluation. Many teachers also have a quick mid-course evaluation they do a third to half-way through the course. The reason for this is then you have an opportunity to make adjustments for the participants over the rest of the course.

A mid-course evaluation should be very short. The essence of it is, "how are we doing so far?" and a number of teachers use that very wording. You can do it as an email or text. You can do it as a group. You can have a half-sheet paper with that question on it.

Surveying Your Participants

Surveys and evaluations often get mixed up and included together. But they are quite different. An evaluation is learner feedback on your course as it was experienced by the person. A survey is feedback on what someone thinks, useful in future offerings.

A survey should be simple and as short as possible. If written, keep the length to one page or less.

Ask questions you really want answered. Change the questions and ask new questions as often as you want, so the survey are always addressing your biggest concerns.

Some things teachers survey their participants about include day, time and location of class meetings, various formats and activities participants might like to see, and topics for future or additional courses.

In general, you only need to ask a question once. For example, if one class likes a break 45 minutes rather than 60 minutes into the class, it is likely future classes will like that as well.

Also, feel free to ask one, two maximum, questions at the start of any or even every class meeting. For example, you could ask "How many of you took the bus or train to class instead of driving? Raise your hands please." You can get good information in just seconds in this way.

Generating Testimonials

Testimonials are helpful not only in promoting your next course, but also in encouraging learners during the course by citing past successful experiences of other participants.

The objective of testimonials is to get a few good ones. You do not need lots of testimonials, only a few outstanding or unique ones.

If you want to generate testimonials for your course, end your course evaluation as we suggested with an open-ended statement like "Other comments:" followed by several blank lines. Then put, "If your comment is a testimonial, can we use it in publicity? _Yes _No"

On the next line put, "If you checked yes, please sign your name

––––––––––

You now have permission to use the testimonial. Save signed testimonials in a file to verify the participant's permission if that is ever needed.[2]

You Can Evaluate Yourself

You can evaluate yourself as a teacher. Author Russell Robinson offers two ways in which to evaluate yourself. One is by habitual but unorganized introspection, or just sitting down and thinking about what you are doing. Another way is to rate your own performance by means of a list of questions or items you deem most important to your teaching and subject matter.[3]

A good time to evaluate yourself is immediately after the class ends. When you are alone, review what went on during class, what went right, what went wrong or could be improved, and how you could change the next class to be better.

Part IV.
Teaching Adults in Higher Education

Chapter 14.
How Younger People Learn Differently

In this section we explore how those of us who teach in higher education can help our students to learn more and complete more. This is now an urgent and compelling need in higher education. In the United States the miserable 55 percent completion rate means that only a little more than one out of every two students completes her or his program of study. In this century, society needs a more educated workforce to keep up with the demands and needs of the information age.

There is much we as instructors can do, without any additional cost and without much, if any, additional time. What we know is that we as teachers have to, and can, do things differently if we are to get a different, and better, result.

At the same time, most students in higher education are now non-traditional students, what some educators call post-traditional students. Most college students, even those of traditional college age, have jobs, families, and/or apartments. A huge percentage are part-time.

It means that everything in this book is even more relevant to students in higher education than ever before.

First, let's look at how younger adults learn differently. Young people born 1980 and later, in general, have some distinctly different learning attributes than people born before them. Gen Y, born between 1980 and 1999, is the first generation for whom the Internet has always existed in their lives.

Those born after 2000 already have an online aptitudes built into their systems. For those of us who spent most of our lives in the last century, we will want to adopt new ways of thinking about learning and our teaching.

Julie Coates, in her pioneering book *Generational Learning Styles,* says that generations learn differently.[1] There are currently five generations currently engaged in learning: Silent Generation (born 1930-1945), Baby Boomers (1946-1964), Gen X (1965-1979), Gen Y (1980-1999), and Gen Z (2000+).

Gen Y and Gen Z clearly learn differently than Baby Boomers and those in the Silent Generation. Coates says Gen X is a transitional generation and thus has a mix of generational learning styles. Some Gen Xers have the learning values of younger generations, some Gen Xers have the learning values of older generations, and some Gen Xers have a mixture.

Here are some of the leading learning characteristics of Gen Y and Gen Z:

Collaborative learning

What we know is that in this century, a group working together at the same time, either synchronously or asynchronously, can produce more of higher quality, than a single individual can produce.

In the last century, individuals worked essentially alone. They all worked with others of course, in the factory, store, office or other place of work. But "working" was something you did by yourself, not with the help of others.

Collaboration means everyone doing the same job at essentially the same time. In this century the world is so complicated, the competition so intense, specialization and niche fields so numerous, and the problems so huge, that a group can be more productive in many instances than an individual. That is, a group can be more creative, more inventive, more productive and more profitable than a single individual working alone.

Open neighbor tests. My colleague Julie Coates discovered one of the first Gen Y teachers. She was Laura Taylor, then age 24, who taught mathematics at North Carolina State University in Raleigh.[2]

Ms. Taylor gave "open neighbor" tests. You may have heard of "open book" tests, where one can look at the book during the test. You could not look at the book during one of Ms. Taylor's tests. But you could talk to your neighbor.

For many older faculty members, this is called cheating. But Ms. Taylor was a statistician and math teacher. She discovered that when students took open neighbor tests, they did better on the final exams, which were neither open neighbor nor open book, than students who did not take open neighbor tests.

Ms. Taylor believed her job was to teach math. So she employed those techniques, including collaborative test-taking, which would improve the learning and knowledge skills of her students. Open neighbor tests are just one way that collaborative learning can be utilized in the classroom.

Learners create content

In the 21st century, students do not just learn content, they also create content. The web has enabled learners to create content. And Gen Y — interactive, involved, a "do it" generation — can and wants to create content.

Now some of you are reading this and thinking this is relevant and applies to your area of knowledge and teaching. And some of you are reading this and think that this has no relevance or applicability to your subject matter or teaching. You might be teaching basic math, and it is unlikely your students will revise 2+2. You might be teaching the history of World War II, and it is unlikely your learners will change the outcome of the Battle of the Bulge.

But creating content does not simply mean creating original new content, although it certainly includes the creation of new ideas and original content. Involving your learners in creating content can have these positive variations.

Learning from your students

Good teachers always learn something from their participants. In the 21st century, learning from your participants may be a prerequisite to good teaching.[3]

We know that anyone born before 1980 can benefit from learning about technology and the Internet from younger people. Not only that, but by the time an older person learns a particular technology, the younger person has already learned two to three times as much. Donald Tapscott, in his book *Growing Up Digital*, calls this "lapping." Most older people will never be able to catch up technology-wise to younger people.[4]

Gen Y teachers and all teachers in the 21st century will benefit from learning from the kids. Respect for the elders in the community has been a traditional value for centuries. But there is also an Ojibway saying: "Respect the young people because they are closer in time to the Creator."

Peak learning time

Learning and teaching becomes a 24-hour activity every day in this century. Schools will need to be open 18 hours a day for both pedagogical and financial reasons. But students will be learning anytime day or night, and teachers will be "on the job" and "on the clock" 24 hours a day.

In this century, we know that people do not all have the same peak work or learning time. Peak work or learning time is the hour or hours of the day or night when a person is most productive, when his or her mind functions best, when both the quantity and quality of work or learning is better than if performed at another time of day or night.

A study of when people said they were most productive revealed the fascinating details. Some 50 percent of people say they are most productive in the morning. Another 25 percent of people say they are most productive in the afternoon. But fully 20 percent of people say they are most productive in the evening, after the typical work day ends. And then 6 percent of people (numbers are rounded) say they are most productive in the night-time hours. The end result will be that peak learning time will enhance each and every student's academic performance.

Self-discipline

One of the critical skills those working in the 21st century will need to have is self-discipline. In knowledge work, there are few supervisors. In the workplace, "supervisor" is a job title that is a relic of the last century. Knowledge workers have to be self-disciplined enough to meet deadlines, meet quality standards, and motivate themselves.

Can teachers who have always had supervisors teach self-discipline and judgment skills to students who will never have supervisors? Individuals in this century will learn self-discipline and judgment skills because they are absolutely essential in the workplace. As teachers we can help, but we cannot supervise.

One of the ways in which we help children and youth with self-discipline is to give them control over increasing amounts of their own time. Another way will be to give them control over their own decision-making.

Every Student is Treated Differently

In the last century, educators believed that equal treatment meant treating each student the same. In this century, teachers and institutions will treat each student differently, not the same. If each of us is different (we are), then as learners we should each be treated differently in order to maximize our learning and our skills. Currently, educators proudly proclaim "We treat each student the same." Treating students the same is supposed to ensure that students are treated equally. And that made sense when students were being prepared for the factory, where all the workers were, and had to be, treated the same.

In this century treating students the same means treating them unequally, not equally. Now treating students equally means treating them differently, not the same. Treating a student with autism the same as a student without autism makes no sense. Likewise, it makes no pedagogical sense to treat a student who excels in math and is three stages ahead of other students of the same age the same as treating a student who needs assistance and is three stages behind other students of the same age.

One way we will treat students differently is to have a learning contract, such as the one advocated for adults by Malcolm Knowles.[5] In schools today educators have an IEP, or individualized education plan, mandated by the Individuals with Disabilities Act. With no one being normal, and every person having one or more weaknesses, think of a learning contract as an IEP for every student.

Peer engagement

The concept of peer engagement is that learners help each other to learn. This concept goes back more than a hundred years in formal schools. In the rural one-room schoolhouse, the teacher would ask older students to help younger ones with their studies.

In today's class, we also have people of differing abilities, levels of achievement and accomplishment. The range may not be as great as the one-through-eighth grade situation, yet in every class some students are ahead of others, some are a little behind, one or two may be way ahead, and one or two way behind.

We clearly cannot continue to categorize learners as "normal" and fitting the norm, and those at either end who do not fit. That view of our students worked when preparing or returning to the factory, but no longer. As teachers, we now need to see this variation as a positive and a learning resource.

Rework is encouraged

In this century, rework will be encouraged and be a standard and accepted way of learning. Taking a test more than once, doing homework over a second time, revising an essay, and engaging in a project a second or even third time currently is not rewarded. Rework is frequently not even allowed. We know, however, that people learn by failure. We know that in this century the objective is not to compare one person to another, but to reach a benchmark. We know "practice makes perfect." In our schools and colleges rework must be common, normal, accepted and encouraged.

'You can't give up on them, says educational administrator Renald Cousineau. 'I see it as a moral imperative not to give up on students.'"[6]

Chapter 15.
Enabling Learning and Completion

"Computers are useless. All they can give you are answers."

— Pablo Picasso, famous modern artist

Most of us as instructors have to get better at enabling learning and completion. The reason is quite simple: in the United States institutions of higher education have a miserable, and unacceptable, rate of completion of just 55 percent. That is failing, failing our students, failing financially and failing society economically.

As a result, America has a shortage of over ten million educated skilled workers. In Canada, the UK and other post industrial nations, the challenge is the same: to have 50 percent of our youth possess a four year undergraduate degree so they can fill the knowledge jobs that make and keep a post-industrial country prosperous.

Here is a true example of how an instructor failed to enable learning and completion.

Willie signed up for a course at his college. The teacher did not tell the students until the first day of the course what the textbook was for the course (first mistake). Willie then found out that the college bookstore did not have the textbook. On the second day of the course the teacher gave an assignment, which involved the textbook, due on Friday (second mistake). The teacher also said no late work, no excuses (third and worst mistake). On

137

the third day of the course Willie was forced to accept his only reasonable option, and he dropped the course.

Afterwards I wondered how much more it would have cost the college, cost the taxpayers, cost society for students like Willie to have completed that course, or any other course. The student had gone through student advising, registration, orientation, tuition payment, enrollment, and online classroom invitation and records. My guess it would have cost the college, taxpayers and society zero dollars, nothing extra, for him, or any other student forced to drop a course, to complete.

We noted at least three unacceptable teaching practices and policies in this real-life true illustration. But in addition, there is also the unacceptable financial waste.

Now here's a positive illustration of enabling learning and completion.

Willie was doing well in his college math class, right up until a week before the final exam, when his best friend died suddenly. Willie did not want to tell his instructor, because in middle school when his mother was diagnosed with cancer and he was worried about losing his mother, his teacher said no late work, no excuses. But he finally emailed his instructor with the message, "Something has come up." His math instructor emailed back, "Well, this better be more important than math." Willie then visited the instructor in-person and explained the situation. And then his math teacher said and did something amazing, something wonderful, and something that is unfortunately all too uncommon. His teacher said, "This is more important than math." With that one simple sentence Willie was given permission to grieve for his best friend and attend the funeral. Neurologically, what happened was that the student's limbic system in the brain was settled and assured and felt 'safe,' knowing that grieving for his friend was seen by his teacher as important. And then, and only because of that one simple sentence and action from his teacher, Willie was able to do what you know is coming next: he not only completed the course by taking the final exam, he aced the final exam.

Our jobs as online instructors are changing from pedagogy to andragogy. Pedagogy is the study and practice of teaching. Andragogy is the study and practice of how we learn. The educational cliché, which is more often said than practiced, is that we have to move from being the sage on the stage to being the guide on the side. But behind the saying are a set of actual teaching practices we have to stop; and actual teaching practices we have to start.

We have to change the predominant teaching style.

Here's a positive illustration of how we can change our obsolete practices and habits and enable learning and completion.

Lynn Mack, in addition to her administrative responsibilities as Dean of Instructional and Grant Development, taught a math class at Piedmont Technical College in South Carolina. An African American young man failed to show up for the final exam. But Lynn Mack really wanted him to pass, so she took the exam to the testing center and told them if he shows up within a week to give him the exam. The testing center called two weeks later and said the young man was there. Just give him the test, Lynn Mack said. The young man took the test and got a 94. He aced the exam! Now 99 percent of faculty probably would have flunked him, but Lynn Mack helped him to complete with no cost to the college and no negative impact on anyone, with a simple time extension. Society needs people with good math skills, not to mention more African American graduates, not to mention more male graduates. In enabling the young man to complete Lynn Mack not only served the student but society and certainly taxpayers.

We can do this. We can enable learning and increase completion rates. And most of it can be accomplished with little or no additional time or effort involved on your part, and little or no cost to your institution and society.

Stop

Here are some of the things we can stop doing and enable learning and completion.

Stop Stressing out students. Julie Coates analyzed the memories of the 1971 class at Carleton College, arguably people from an elite college where one has to be academically successful just to get admitted. Coates found the most common memory was nightmares about school and college. That suggests students are being stressed in school and college, even more than at work. As we have noted earlier, neuroscientists say increasing a student's stress level inhibits learning. Stress in no way motivates someone to learn. Stress prevents learning.

Stop disrespecting students. From comments faculty make in our online courses over the last ten years, we estimate that only about 15 percent of teachers disrespect their students. Most faculty respect their students. And yet the 15 percent of teachers who disrespect their students is way too high, meaning that a student will encounter such a teacher in 1 of every 7 courses.

Administrators clearly need to tell all faculty that it is simply unacceptable for faculty to disrespect their students.

Stop preparing students for the 'real world.' You and I, if you were born before 1980, have no idea what the real world will be like for our young people. For example, if you think your students will need to "show up on time" at work, you are wrong. Employers and your students know telework is on the increase, teleworkers are 25 percent more productive than office workers, and that companies are more profitable when people work at their own peak work time, not during specified hours. You and I understand the real world of the last century, not this century.

Stop preparing students for the workplace. Most often instructors use this phrase and the accompanying set of bad instructional techniques as an excuse for poor teaching. There's no big problem in the workplace society needs you to solve, that you can solve.

There's no big problem with irresponsible engineers in the workplace. The big problem is we don't have enough engineers in the workplace.

Stop penalizing your students, which is gender biased, for turning in work late. There's no problem with males showing up on time in the workplace, and there's no problem with males turning their work in on time. Ask any employer (we did) and she will say male employees perform at the same level as female employees.

Stop policies that prevent or inhibit learning. Many policies are carry overs from the last century. They are designed either to serve the interests of the institution, or to actually help weed out students from completion. Some policies get created for that once-in-a-lifetime incidence and hurt everyone else. Other policies can be replaced by technology. Policies can be changed without cost and without time.

Stop punishing students for behavior. Behavior has nothing to do with learning and knowledge. By punishing students for behavior, we deprive society of valuable business people, professionals and leaders. If Winston Churchill had been prevented from attending university because of his behavior, who would have won WWII? Thousands of people owe their lives

140

to the work of Robert Oppenheimer, who actually tried to poison his teacher in college, but was given probation and counseling rather than expulsion. Mark Zuckerberg was forced out of college for behavior and made it. But what about the thousands of other students forced out for behavior who could otherwise now be scientists, technology professionals, engineers, and mathematicians?

Stop justifying bad teaching by blaming students. Faculty have not been trained to do what they do every day — teach. The emerging field of faculty development is here to stay. Each of us as teachers needs to keep learning about effective teaching techniques. The time is coming when governments and societies will enforce teacher accountability. And if you and I continue our professional development, we have nothing to worry about.

Stop treating students like military recruits. Treat your students as both adults and children. Treat them with respect as adults, and with care as children.

- If a student is under the age of 30, she, and more likely he, still is not neurologically mature, there are still synapses that simply and biologically have not, and cannot, be connected yet.

- Students of any age will have feelings of inadequacy and less than a positive self-image, and part of your job is to make every student of every age feel able to learn. Take care of your students.

- Not so long ago colleges understood they needed to take care of their students, with 'en loco parentis,' fulfilling the role of parents. Even in a world, back then, when most 18-year-olds went to work rather than to college, when age 18 was the age of majority, colleges understood they needed to take care of their students as a parent would.

And treat your students with respect as adults. Many if not most of even young students have part time jobs, some family responsibilities. Some are asked to fight, many are asked to vote. They deserve to have their thoughts and opinions respected.

Start

Here are some of the things we can start doing to enable more learning and improve retention and completion rates.

Start treating each student differently. Treating each student the same is to treat them unequally. You treat each student equally when you treat each one differently. It might be different projects, different assessments, and different learning speed. Create a set of options. Be open to responding to each of your students in a way that increases her or his learning.

Start allowing extended time. Extended time, whether for assignments or even tests, is one of the most effective tools at your disposal to increase learning and completion.

Start encouraging students to redo quizzes. Encourage students to take quizzes over until they have mastered the learning.

Start encouraging rework. Encourage and even build-in rework phases in student assignments. We learn by failure. There are some educators who maintain we only learn by failure. Rework enables a student to turn failure into success. The goal is to reach the benchmark and to learn, not weed out or compare.

Start more frequent testing. In the online environment that is easily done with weekly self-graded quizzes.

Start allowing collaboration. Students working with each other, even during tests, has been shown to increase learning. In this century workers who collaborate are more productive, and students who collaborate learn more.

For example, Laura Taylor, as a math instructor at North Carolina State University, had her students do 'open neighbor' tests. While they could not look at the book during the test, they could talk to another student. What Taylor found was that students who did 'open neighbor' tests performed higher in the final exam, which was neither open book nor 'open neighbor,' than students who did not do 'open neighbor' tests.

Give your smart students equal attention. Every student deserves your attention. But most instructors teach to the average, the median, and sometimes even lower.

Yet the big problem in society is we are not graduating enough smart students. Smart students go into STEM. Smart students invent stuff. Smart students hire other people. Your smart students are often overlooked and underserved. Give them the same, but different, attention.

In a recent online course, a faculty member asked for tips on teaching the talented and gifted. Here's what we said.

142

Ramp it up. Make it as intellectually challenging as possible. Smart students thrive on challenging work. Push them intellectually, and let them push you intellectually.

Rely totally on testing, not on homework. No busy work. Smart students want and need the intellectual challenge, but not the boring repetitive simple stuff. Challenging is good, more work is not.

Allow quiz outs. If they know it, let them prove it and move on. We want our smart students to go as far as they can. Let them quiz out and move on to more challenging work.

No penalty for behavior. If you grade based on attendance and penalize for late work and other behavior not related to learning and knowledge, your smart, and really smart, students will drop out, mentally if nothing else. If you would have flunked Steve Jobs, Bill Gates and Mark Zuckerberg, don't even try teaching the gifted and talented.

Let them teach. Let them teach others. Let them share their knowledge. Let them create content. All the research says that we learn more by teaching. And many instructors have reported that the other students benefit from having the smart students share their knowledge as well.

Let them go. Forget your control urges, and if they go off on a tangent, let them. It's called a "teachable moment" when you lose control and it's almost always the most exciting time of the course for both students and you.

Get ready to have a great experience. Teaching smart students is a remarkable and rewarding experience. Enjoy it.

The Top 10 Solutions to increasing completion rates

Inform your institution about our Top 10 Solutions to increasing completion rates. There may be other ways to enable learning and completion, and we would support them as well. These are our Top 10 Solutions, many unique to this author and my colleague Julie Coates, and almost all involving little or no expense on the part of your institution nor little or no additional time on your part as teacher.

1. Make all face-to-face classes hybrid. Every in-person course at your institution should, and eventually will, be hybrid.

2. All assignments are made online. All progress and scores are reported online. Each student has a record online of assignments completed due and completed, as well as grade completion and other progress.

3. No teacher is to express verbally, or in writing, a negative comment about students. This extends to expressing negative comments about students made to other faculty, administrators or any other person in a work or public arena.

4. Increase outcomes, reduce 'work' requirements. Increase assignments and assessments based on learning outcomes, rather than work or time inputs.

5. Do not allow behavior to be a part of grading. This includes attendance and late work.

6. Allow extended time. Allow and encourage extended time for taking tests and turning in assignments and course work.

7. Allow quiz outs. Allow and encourage students to quiz out of Units where they have demonstrated a mastery of the content.

8. Provide alternative assessments. Provide options for assessments, particularly for essays and papers not associated with writing courses.

9. Revise policies. Revise institutional, departmental and other policies which prevent retention and completion.

10. Retakes and transfers at no cost. Any student can retake a course without paying additional tuition. Any student can transfer into another offering of the same course at no additional cost.

Chapter 16.
Gender Differences in Learning

Gender characteristics are tendencies associated with one sex or the other. Scientists say that sex is almost always either/or. One is either male or female. Gender, however, is not either/or, as noted by Dr. Leonard Sax in *Why Gender Matters*. Gender characteristics are tendencies. When we speak of male characteristics or female characteristics, we are talking about tendencies. Not every female student will behave with entirely female characteristics, and not every male student will behave with entirely male characteristics. Nevertheless, most males will exhibit male characteristics, while most females will exhibit female characteristics.

Twenty percent cross-over

The twenty percent cross-over concept is the finding that about 20 percent of one sex will have the characteristic or activity generally associated predominantly of the other sex.[1] There is nothing abnormal in this. It is fascinating that in looking at the statistics for an activity predominantly associated with one sex or the other, the percent of the other sex participating is so often close to 20 percent. For example, a University of Cambridge study found that 17 percent of men have a 'female' empathizing brain and 17 percent of women have a 'male' systemizing brain.

The Impact of Neurological Differences

The human brain becomes masculinized or feminized before birth as a result of being exposed to testosterone and estrogen, among other hormones. If the brain receives more testosterone in utero, it develops into a male brain, and more estrogen will result in a female brain. The hormones are produced by the mother, based on the chromosomal structure of the developing fetus. There is no brain that is wholly masculine or feminine, but there is a huge spectrum of difference between the male and female brains.

What is most important to understand is that there are measurable, quantifiable differences in how most men and women respond to the same stimuli, and this is biologically based, not culturally determined.

The Female Brain

Simon Baron-Cohen in his book, *"The Essential Difference: Men, Women and the Extreme Male Brain,"* notes that there are measurable differences in the brain between females and males. Men have 4% more brain cells than women, and about 100 grams more of brain tissue. Men have more gray matter, but women have more white matter. Women also have more dendritic connections between brain cells. A woman's brain has a larger corpus collusum, which means women can transfer data between the right and left hemisphere faster than men. Some scientists believe that women score higher on spatial memory tests because the larger size of their corpus callosum. Men tend to process more in the left brain while women have greater access to both sides. Women tend to use both sides of the brain to process language while men tend to process more often in the dominant hemisphere - typically the left side. This gives women a distinct advantage in language. Females can process visual and other signals at the same time more easily than men. Women have a larger deep limbic system than men. This gives them the ability to be more in touch with their feelings and to express them than men.[2] Females, for example, score higher than males on tests measuring empathy.

The Male Brain

The male brain triggers behaviors and responses based on its structure and neurochemistry.

The male brain is lower in serotonin, a neurotransmitter that plays an important role in memory, emotion, sleep and wakefulness; lower in oxytocin, a hormone that is important to emotional behavior; a smaller corpus callosum than the female brain and a smaller language center. The amygdala are larger and have fewer neural pathways to the frontal lobes, and a smaller hippocampus with low-range pathways to emotive centers. In the male brain, there is less cross-communication between hemispheres. There are fewer aural neurons, so loud noises are not a problem, for example. And males have significantly more testosterone than females. The male brain triggers behaviors and responses based on its structure and neurochemistry.

The Fundamental Difference

Overall, males and females are equal in intelligence. And they share most intellectual functions in common and to the same level. Young men and young women also test overall at roughly the same level.

But there are two significant differences in cognitive skills that greatly impact the learning of both female and male students.

There is so much scientific evidence, based on neurology and hormonal differences in the brain, that it is both impossible and counterproductive to ignore or rationalize these two differences.

Females are superior in language skills

This includes both verbal and written language skills. It does not mean every female is superior to every male; but overall, most females have superior language skills than most males.

The research suggests that females process language information using both sides of their brain, while males use only one side of the brain. They also process information in different areas of the brain. At the same time, females also have better neural connections between the areas of the brain devoted to emotion and to language, thus making it easier for females to express emotion.

Males are superior in spatial skills

It does not mean every male is superior to every female; but overall, most males have superior spatial skills to that of most females. Doreen Kimura, in

149

her book *"Sex and Cognition,"* cites the evidence that spatial skill is linked to testosterone. She notes that studies have found that males receive three surges in testosterone levels. One surge is before birth, one in infancy, and one in the teen years. After each surge, tests show males spatial skills increase over that of females' spatial skills at the same time.[3]

Standardized tests administered by varying testing agencies over decades show this difference in cognitive skills between females and males on a consistent basis.

Males and Females Test Equally

The scientific evidence about these two significant differences is so compelling, and the implications for enhancing both the learning of your male students and your female students so clear, that we call these two ying-yang variations "The Fundamental Difference" in how and why your male students learn differently than your female students.

As we have just stated, overall, males and females — men and women, young men and young women, boys and girls — are equally intelligent. There is no credible study that shows otherwise. Researchers on gender and intelligence make a point that the two sexes are equal in intelligence.

Equally important, young men and young women also test overall at roughly the same level. In their classic work, *Gender and Fair Assessment,* Educational Testing Service researchers Nancy S. Cole and Warren Willingham state, "Based on a wide variety of tests and a number of large nationally representative samples of high school seniors, we see no evidence of any consequential difference in the average test performance of young women and men."[4]

The Implications for Teachers

For every educator, it is essential to understand that learning happens differently for males and females. Only when this happens, can we as educators assist both our female and male students to learn more and be able to perform optimally in school. The task requires setting aside some of our cultural myths, educating ourselves about the neurology of learning.

Specifically, you need to recognize that males, in general, have higher spatial ability than females; and that females, in general, have higher language ability than males. You need to be gender neutral in your teaching, developing specific strategies to create a more comfortable environment for learning for both our male and female students. And you need to make sure you are gender neutral in your grading, as males and females test equally overall at all levels in education.

Chapter 17.
Grading in the 21st Century

The way teachers grade has to be changed. To be blunt, if you are a teacher in higher education, you get an F in your correctness in grading. Faculty grade a student appropriately less than 50 percent of the time, according to a study by Nancy Cole, who was then president of the Educational Testing Service, and Warren Willingham. That's failing. You and other instructors get an F in grading your students.

According to their study, based on thousands of tests and millions of students, female students are given a grade commensurate with their test scores about 47 percent of the time, and male students just 44 percent of the time. About 28 percent of students, 33 percent of females and 20 percent of males, are given grades significantly higher than what their test scores indicate they know and have learned. And another 28 percent, some 36 percent of males and 20 percent of females, are given significantly worse grades than what they have learned and know.[1]

In this chapter we explore how grading is changing in the 21st century and what you can do now in your online course to give your students grades more appropriate to their learning and knowledge.

1. Measure outcomes not time

Measuring time is now obsolete. In the first two decades of the 20th century, the current system of grading and assessment was created largely in response to the need for education to prepare students for work and life in the factory and office.

The Carnegie Foundation took a leading role in the creation of time as a measurement of educational attainment. By 1910, nearly all secondary institutions in the United States used the "Carnegie Unit" as a measure of secondary course work.

The Carnegie Foundation contracted with Morris Llewellyn Cooke to explore ways to measure education at the higher education level. His resulting work, "Academic and Industrial Efficiency," was published in 1910 and became the basis for the Student Hour used by colleges and universities.

Again, the motive here was to standardize educational measurement and faculty workloads. Cooke established the collegiate Student Hour as "an hour of lecture, of lab work, or of recitation room work, for a single pupil."

Today your students are not going into the factory, and they will be evaluated by their employers based on their outcomes and productivity, not on time input. In fact, in this century workers are rewarded when they spend less time getting a desired outcome, not more time.

What you can do as an online instructor is to evaluate your students based on their learning outcomes, not by the amount of time they put in.

2. No grading on the curve

Grades also served the interests of the factory, and helped solidify the factory school model of the last century.

The grading system of A (excellent), B (good), C (average), D (below average) and F (failure) was based not on objective scores, but on a comparison with other students (sometimes referred to by students as "the curve").

This was helpful to the factory, where a major personnel issue was the assignment of people to various levels of jobs within the factory. Thus, a student who was a "C" student, and thus average, became a factory worker on the assembly line. A student who was a "B" student and above was more likely to be able to become a foreman or supervisor in the factory. And the "A" or excellent students went on to college and became the managers and professionals in the factory and office.

In terms of college and university, society deemed that only around 25 percent of our nation's youth needed to be college graduates, and thus part of higher education's mission in the last century was to keep 75 percent of the youth out of college.

Today the objective of higher education is not to keep people out of college, but to get as many as possible to complete. We need everyone to know English, everyone to be able to do math.

In your online course, set a benchmark for passing and help all of your students to complete and succeed.

3. Enact Gender Neutral Grading

Since 1980, higher education has had a gender bias against males. The result is that millions of smart males — a smart male is one who tests at the same or higher level as those in college — are not admitted, are not retained, and are not graduated from college. And in every college and university, males are given lower grades than females even though they learn as much.

The consequence of what a recent OECD study called "The Reversal of Gender Inequalities in Higher Education," (See The Reversal of Gender Inequalities in Higher Education: An On-going Trend, by Stéphan Vincent-Lancrin, Higher Education to 2030, OECD, 2008, ISBN 978-92-64-04065-6) has created a crisis in society.[2] It has resulted in millions of smart students not being admitted to college, not being graduated, and not being admitted into graduate school. Consequently, in the United States we will have a shortage of 14 million skilled workers by 2017, according to Anthony Carnevale, the nation's leading training researcher.

The shortage is particularly acute among science, technology, engineering and math professions, the now well-known acronym STEM, as STEM professionals are central to a post-industrial economic and social prosperity for advanced countries.

The consequences of graduating millions of mediocre students and sending millions of our smartest students to Walmart and McDonald's is now staggering and economically unsustainable.

What we know is that male and female students test equally. We know males learn as much as females. And Richard Arum's classic study, *Academically Adrift,* found that graduating males tested at the same level as females and had the same level of success in the workplace several years later.[3] And yet even the highest achieving males in the top quintile of both work success and testing scores were given grades lower than females with the same test scores. Faculty and institutions have to follow Title IX, which prohibits discrimination on the basis of gender.

The bottom line is that you have to stop your gender bias in grading, and start grading on a gender neutral basis.

4. Test when ready

Tests will be given when the student is ready to take the test. As Mike Baker, Education Editor for BBC News writes, "Instead of preparing pupils for the high stakes tests at the end of each key stage, teachers' focus would be on assessing when a child is able to move up one level in the national curriculum grades. When they think a child is ready, they can put them in for a test that will be set and marked outside the school. They will not have to wait, as now, until pupils reach the end of a key stage at seven, 11 or 14. This will mean 'several shorter, more focused, and more appropriate tests' for each child, rather than one big test at the end of the key stage.[4]

5. Grade learning, not behavior

An immediate problem in education is to eliminate grading based on behavior. All students should be graded solely on their learning and knowledge, not behavior. Grading based on behavior has detrimental effects for both female students and male students.

Currently grading is not based solely on learning and knowledge. Instead, grades are assigned to a great extent by behavior instead of learning and knowledge.

Graded behavior includes:

• Attendance.

• Turning homework and coursework in late.

• Not doing assigned homework or coursework.

• Taking exams and tests late.

• Behavior deemed inappropriate by school authorities.

You are not teaching responsibility, otherwise the gender GPA gap would close over time. And you are not preparing your students for the workforce, because studies show that males are very responsible in the work place.

The role of schools and colleges in the 21st century is purely, entirely and totally about learning and knowledge, not about behavior. There are no beneficial effects from including behavior in grading. The negative effects are numerous and troubling.

In summarizing grading and assessment for the 21st century, the way learners are assessed in this century needs to be transformed. Focus your grading and assessment only on learning and knowledge. Make your testing and assessment more objective, exclude behavior as a criterion, and employ multiple assessments. Pedagogically, best of all better grading and assessment becomes integrally part of the learning process. Good assessment doesn't just measure learning but actually enhances each student's learning.

Chapter 18.
Summary

When this author was in second grade, the teacher, Eileen Hargrove, put all assignments aside every Friday afternoon and read to us from the book *Lazy Liza Lizard*. Ever since then, Friday has been my favorite day of the week. I have fragmented memories of the joys of listening to Miss Hargrove read those stories.

A few years ago, I decided to get a copy of *Lazy Liza Lizard* and reread those wonderful tales. The public library did not have it, the Bragg Elementary School did not have it, and even Miss Hargrove did not have it. After searching antique shops and rummage sales, I began embarrassing myself by asking every parent, children's librarian, or publisher if they had ever heard of *Lazy Liza Lizard*. My mother, who runs a large used book sale every year, joined me in the search. She also wrote to rare book dealers around the country inquiring for me. Four years later, a rare book dealer in Massachusetts sent the book to me, and I eagerly opened it up and read the first five stories.

To my immediate disappointment, they were all the same. Lazy Liza was not nearly so exciting a personality as I had recalled, and the book was quickly put down.

It was only then that it occurred to me that what made Lazy Liza so fascinating, what made Fridays my favorite day ever since second grade, was not the book, nor the reading, nor the day, but Miss Hargrove. She made those things come alive, and she was the reason I remembered them so well.

Like my second grade classroom, the most important thing in your class is you, the teacher. Ultimately, no media trick or interaction technique will make or break your class. You are the single most important link between your learners and what they want to learn. Your excitement, your pleasantness, your interest, enthusiasm, your enjoyment of the experience will make the difference for your participants. They will have gained something because of you. I hope they will not have missed out on something because of you.

In this short book, I have tried to put together the most successful practices now known in helping to teach adults. Whether you read the book, skimmed it, or even just glanced at it is not important. What is important is if you gained even one tip which will improve your class, making you a better teacher and helping your participants to learn more.

As we enter into the area of lifelong learning, it will become increasingly critical that each of us learn continually to keep up in our jobs, grow personally, and be better citizens. You can help in your role as a teacher. By viewing your teaching as a mutual sharing of ideas, experiences, and warmth, you can demonstrate that the best teacher is the one who continues to learn from his or her students. You can help make your class a rich, stimulating, and involving interaction; you can help make lifelong learning the same.

One of the greatest joys in teaching is seeing the sparkle in someone's eyes, the delight in discovering something new, the warmth in making a new friend, establishing a new friendship, the opportunity to express oneself. You can join thousands of others in one of the exciting challenges of this century, helping to make us truly a nation of learners.

In these pages, I attempted to show you how to plan better, teach, and improve your class. We talked about how adults learn, stressing the critical factors of self-image and past experiences, and how you can help your students learn better by listening, by helping insecure learners, by avoiding punishment actions, by providing supportive actions, and by adding a touch of humor.

There are four things you, as a teacher of adults must do to have a successful teaching experience. To describe them, I have developed the scheme **DIVE,** as in "dive or plunge into your teaching." The formula is: Discover your participants, Involve your participants, Vary your teaching techniques, Energize your learning environment.

In preparing your course, think about how to:

- Set a positive learning climate the first class meeting by getting to know the participants and having them get to know each other.
- Use your participants' experiences and knowledge throughout the class.
- Call on a variety of teaching techniques in assisting you to convey your message each class.
- Ask for critical feedback so you can improve your class for the next time.

Teaching adults is both a serious business and fun. I hope you enjoy it. And perhaps you will remain as alive and rich in your experience as the senior citizen I once met in our building.

One night at work, I wearily went down to the basement to buy a soft drink from the vending machine. There I met an elderly man standing around, obviously waiting for an evening class to begin. "Are you a student or the teacher?" I asked, not wanting to offend him either way. "Well, I suppose I'm the teacher," the man replied, "but I'm always learning, too."

Appendix
Writing Course Descriptions

If you are offering a course that will be publicized through a catalog or brochure, you or the course sponsor will need to write a course description. The course description is vital to getting people to enroll in your course. A good course description can mean many enrollments while a poor course description can doom your course before it starts. Ideally, you should work with your class sponsor in writing the course description and then follow these guidelines.

Many, if not most, course descriptions are repetitive, dull or grammatically sloppy. If people do not read your course description, they will not take your course.

The course description is made up of these items:

A. Title

B. Course Description

C. Logistics

D. Teacher Biography

Title

The title should be simple or catchy. Long or complex titles tend to confuse, and dull titles will not capture the reader's eye. Generally, for skill classes such as home repair or the arts, you will want a simple title. For idea classes such as interpersonal relations and social issues, catchy titles will attract the reader, turning an average or dull topic into an interesting one.

Here are some good course titles:

- "Stained Glass" (simple)
- "101 Uses for a Dead Poet" (catchy)

Course Description

Every course description should have these elements:

- It should be enticing or interesting.
- It should be factually complete and accurate.
- It should have solid course information.

Every newspaper has to have the five Ws: Who, What, Where, When, Why. Your job in writing a course description is much easier, since Where and When are in the logistics section, and Who is irrelevant or a useless gesture don't write, "Everyone should take this course."

Here are a few guidelines for the description:

1. The description should be 40 words to 120 words in length. Fewer than 40 is too sketchy; more than 120 is too long.
2. The description should be divided into two paragraphs if it is more than 60 words. More than 60 words in one paragraph is hard to read.
3. The teacher biography or qualifications should not be mixed in with the course description.
4. Do not use abbreviations unless everyone knows what they stand for.
5. Write in complete sentences. Incomplete sentences should be used infrequently and only for emphasis.

Your description should focus on the content of the course or the learner, not on the course itself or you as the teacher. To attract learners, the description should emphasize the benefits to the learner coming from either the results of attending the course or from the value of the subject matter itself. Learners are interested in themselves and in the content of the course, not in the course itself or the teacher.

In general, the first one or two sentences should be enticing, dramatic, or otherwise interesting. The following two to five sentences should be a summary of the scope of the content of the course.

The first five words of the description will often determine if the reader will go on to pass to another course description.

Here are six good opener techniques:

1. A definition
2. The end result
3. The outstanding or impressive fact
4. A question
5. The quotation
6. The distraction

Definitions, end results and impressive facts are used frequently in course descriptions. Questions, quotations or distractions are used sparingly.

Here are some poor openers:

• The aim of this course is to .... (Course oriented)

• Shirley has been teaching ballet for two years now. (Teacher oriented)

• This class will .... (Focus on course)

• The teacher will explain .... (Focus on teacher) Here are some good openers:

• Batik is an age-old sort of fabric coloring using wax and dye. (Definition)

• Effective fiction enables the reader to live a story as if it's his or her own life. (End result)

• You can be a moral person without following traditional religions. (End result)

• Baffled, bored, or intimidated by opera? (The question)

• Lighting is the key to all photography. (Outstanding fact)

• No man is an island. (Quotation)

• Does your life seem like a soap opera? (A question)

• Grr. Hold it Horace! Don't throw that pillow yet. (Distraction)

• Fred Astaire, Ginger Rogers, Gene Kelly and you. (Content and end result, excellent enticer)

Describe outcomes. Either in your opening sentence, or immediately following, describe the outcomes for the learner of your course.

Your potential participants are very interested in what they will be able to do or know after your course is over. Most people are less interested in what will happen during your course.

Stress the benefits, outcomes and end results of participating in your course.

Use active verbs. Use one or more active verbs to describe the outcomes of your course. When you use active verbs, the outcomes are even more appealing. Some active verbs to use:

- Discover ...
- Acquire...
- Take home...
- Get. ..
- Learn ...
- Take away ...

Use the second person. When writing your course description, use the second person or "you" language. Do not use the third person "Participants will," or the first person "I will."

Instead of saying "Participants will acquire valuable ideas" say "You will acquire valuable ideas."

Logistics

Logistics include the teacher's name, class location, day, length, cost, material fees, course number and other adjunct information. The course sponsor normally provides this information, although you should be aware of all information pertinent to your class.

Teacher Biography

The teacher biography should be 15 to 50 words in a separate paragraph underneath the course description. Some organizations will run all of their teacher biographies at the end of the catalog.

The biography should have two seemingly contradictory goals: 1) to establish you as qualified; 2) to project your image as a peer, not too far above potential learners. Learners want to know you are qualified, but they also want someone who can relate to them.

Your qualifications should be stated in terms of experience. Use credentials or degrees only as a last resort. By including your interest or motivation in teaching the course, the participants will also see you as a likable peer.

Further Reading

Generational Learning Styles, by Julie Coates

Learn more about your students. Discover something new about yourself. Different generations have different ways of learning. Find out the implications for your teaching. Take home practical, how-to tips for teaching Seniors, Baby Boomers, Gen Xers, and Gen Y learners.

Education in the 21st Century, by William A. Draves and Julie Coates

Our current educational system, which has served society so well for the past 100 years, is now obsolete. While our schools and colleges cannot be fixed, they can and are being transformed into a more relevant educational system.

We provide a new model for education, including a new mission, curriculum, grading, and financial structure, plus the 21 pedagogical concepts for the 21st century, and a section on personalizing teaching to help every student.

Nine Shift: Work, life and education in the 21st century, by William A. Draves and Julie Coates

In just twenty years, between 2000 and 2020, some 75 percent of our lives will change dramatically. We know this because it happened once before. Between 1900 and 1920, life changed.

Discover each of the major nine shifts currently taking place, and find out the implications of each shift for business and work, life and education.

"Fascinating." —BBC

"A most interesting book."—Peter Drucker

Advanced Teaching Online, by William A. Draves

Some half of all learning will be online in this century. The opportunities are tremendous for teaching online. Find out how to plan, develop and teach an online course. Relevant for both those new to teaching online, and experienced online teachers who want advanced tips to take their teaching to the next level.

More than 6,000 teachers have taken the author's online course.

Books available from LERN. For information and to order:
• Call 800-678-5376.
• Email info@lern.org.
• Visit www.lern.org.

Bibliography

Apps, Jerold W., *Mastering the Teaching of Adults*, Krieger Publishing, Malabar, Florida, 1991.

Bischof, Ledford J. *Adult Psychology*, Harper & Row, Publishers: New York, 1969.

Brookfield, Stephen, *The Skillful Teacher*, Jossey-Bass Publishers: San Francisco, 1990.

Brookfield, Stephen D., and Preskill, Stephen, *Discussion As a Way of Teaching*, Jossey-Bass, San Francisco, 1999.

Caffarella, Rosemary and Merriam, Sharan, *Learning in Adulthood*, Jossey-Bass Publishers: San Francisco, 1991.

Candy, Phillip C., *Self-Direction for Lifelong Learning*, Jossey Bass Publishers: San Francisco, 1991.

Coates, Julie, *Generational Learning Styles*, Learning Resources Network, River Falls, WI, 2007.

Conrad, Rita-Marie and Donaldson, J. Ana, *Engaging the Online Learner*, Jossey-Bass, San Francisco, 2004.

Daloz, Laurent, *Effective Teaching and Mentoring*, Jossey-Bass Publishers: San Francisco, 1986.

Dereshiwsky, Mary, *Continual Engagement: Fostering Online Discussion*, Learning Resources Network: River Falls, WI, 2013.

Dickenson, Gary, *Teaching Adults: A Handbook for Instructors*, General Publishing Co. Limited: Don Mills, Ontario, 1973.

Draves, William A. and Coates, Julie, *The Pedagogy of the 21st Century*, Learning Resources Network: River Falls, WI, 2011.

Draves, William A. and Coates, Julie, *Nine Shift: Work, life and educa-*

tion in the 21" century, Learning Resources Network: River Falls, WI, 2004.

Draves, William A, *Advanced Teaching Online,* Learning Resources Network: River Falls, WI, 2014.

Draves, Willaim A., *Energizing the Learning Environment,* Learning Resources Network: Manhattan, Kansas, 1995.

Eble, Kenneth, *The Craft of Teaching,* second edition, Jossey-Bass Publishers: San Francisco, 1988.

Freire, Paulo, *Pedagogy of the Oppressed,* Herder and Herder: New York, 1972.

Grabowski, Stanley M., *Training Teachers of Adults: Models and Innovative Programs,* Syracuse University: Syracuse, NY, 1976.

Gurian, Michael, *Boys and Girls Learn Differently,* Jossey-Bass: San Francisco, 2003.

Highet, Gilbert, *The Art of Teaching,* Vintage Books: New York, 1954.

Illich, Ivan, *Deschooling Society,* Harper & Row, Publishers: New York, 1970.

Ilsley, Paul J., and Niemi, John A., *Recruiting and Training Volunteers,* McGraw-Hill Book Company: New York, 1981.

Kidd, J. R., *How Adults Learn,* Association Press: New York, 1973, 1959.

Knowles, Malcolm, *Self-Directed Learning,* Follet Publishing Company: Chicago, 1980.

Knowles, Malcolm, *The Adult Learner: A Neglected Species,* Gulf Publishing Company: Houston, 1973.

Knowles, Malcolm, *The Modern Practice of Adult Education,* Follet Publishing Company: Chicago, 1980.

Mills, H. R., *Teaching and Training: A Handbook for Instructors,* John Wiley & Sons: New York, 1977.

Nadler, Leonard, *Developing Human Resources,* Gulf Publishing Company: Houston, 1970.

Nelson, Florence, *Yes, You Can Teach!* Carma Press: St. Paul, MN, 1977.

Reimer, Everett, *School is Dead,* Doubleday & Company: Garden City, New York, 1972.

Robinson, Russell D., *Helping Adults Learn and Change,* Omnibook Company: Milwaukee, 1979.

Smith, Robert M., *Learning How to Learn: Applied Theory for Adults,*

Follett Publishing Company: Chicago, 1982.

Smith, Robert M. and Associates, *Learning to Learn Across the Life Span,* Jossey-Bass Publishers: San Francisco, 1990.

Srinivasan, Lyra, *Perspectives on Nonformal Adult Learning,* World Education: New York, 1979.

Tough, Allen, *The Adult's Learning Projects,* The Ontario Institute for Studies in Education: Toronto, 1971.

Vella, Jane, *Training Through Dialogue,* Jossey-Bass Publishers: San Francisco, 1995.

Verduin, John R., Miller, Harry G., and Greer, Charles E., *Adults Teaching Adults,* Learning Concepts: Austin, TX, 1977.

Willingham, Warren W., and Cole, Nancy S., *Gender and Fair Assessment,* Lawrence Erlbaum Associates: Mahwah, NJ, 1997.

Notes

Chapter 2.

[1]J. Roby Kidd, *How Adults Learn* (New York, NY: Association Press, 1973, 1959), page #95.

[2]Ronald Gross, *Invitation to Lifelong Learning,* Chicago, IL: Follett Publishing Company, 1982), pg 48.

[3]Kidd, Page 95.

[4]Sharon Merriam and Rosemary Cafarella, *Learning in Adulthood* (San Francisco, CA: Jossey-Bass Publishers, 1991), page 307.

[5]Draves, William, and Coates, Julie, *The Pedagogy of the 21st Century,* River Falls, WI, LERN Books, 2011

[6]See the work of Dr. Eric H. Chudler, University of Washington

[7]Coates, Julie, *Generational Learning Styles,* River Falls, WI, LERN Books, 2007.

[8]James Zull keynote, 28th Annual Conference on Distance Teaching & Learning, August 9, 2012, University of Wisconsin, Madison, Wisconsin.

[9]Laurent A. Daloz, *Effective Teaching and Mentoring* (San Francisco, CA: Jossey-Bass Publishers, 1986), page 157.

Chapter 3.

[1]Kenneth Eble, *The Craft of Teaching,* second edition, (San Francisco, CA: Jossey-Bass Publishers, 1988)

[2]Russell Robinson, *Helping Adults Learn and Change* (Milwaukee, WI: Omnibook Company, 1979), page 50.

[3]Stephen Brookfield, *The Skillful Teacher* (San Francisco, CA: Jossey-

Bass Publishers, 1990), Page 94.

[4]Robinson, page 52.

[5]Phillip C. Candy, *Self-Direction for Lifelong Learning* (San Francisco, CA: Jossey-Bass Publishers, 1991), page 391.

[6]Robinson, Page 56.

[7]Ibid

[8]Ibid

[9]Florence Nelson, *Yes, You Can Teach* (St. Paul, MN: Carma Press, 1977), page 30.

Chapter 4.

[1]Michael Gurian, *Boys and Girls Learn Differently* (San Francisco, Jossey-Bass, 2001).

See also: Brain Based Learning, by Jeb P. Schenck, Wyoming Community Education Association Conference, Jackson, WY, 2005.

Teaching with the Brain in Mind, by Eric Jensen, Alexandria, VA: Association for Supervision and Curriculum Development, 2005.

[2]Warren W. Willingham and Nancy S. Cole, *Gender and Fair Assessment* (Mahwah, NJ, Lawrence Erlbaum Associates, 1997), pages 68-69.

[3]Julie Coates, *Generational Learning Styles* (River Falls, Wisconsin, Learning Resources Network, 2007).

Chapter 5

[1]The "glob" quote is from "Customizing the Learning Experience with Reusable Content Objects," by Susan Kirshbaum, speech, LearningByte International seminar, April 23, 2000, St. Paul, Minnesota.

[2]Weydauer's comments are from his keynote address, LERN's Learning Online 2001 conference, June 25, 2001, Minneapolis.

[3]"All teaching becomes publishing" is from a Copyright and Intellectual Property panel discussion, World Education Market conference, Vancouver, Canada, May 24-26, 2001.

Chapter 6

[1]John R Verduin, Harry G. Miller, and Charles E Greer, *Adults Teaching Adults* (Austin, TX: Learning Concepts, 1977), pages 84-88.

[2]Tim Wentling, *Planning for Effective Training* (Rome, Italy: Food an Agriculture Organization of the United Nations, 1993), pages 101-109.

Chapter 7

[1]The term "web enhanced" courses is from *The Online Teaching Survival Guide,* by Judith V. Boettcher and Rita-Marie Conrad, Jossey Bass, 2010

[2]The best book on integrative learning and in-person teaching is *Mastering the Teaching of Adults by Jerold Apps,* Krieger Publishing, Melbourne, Florida, 1991.

Chapter 8

[1]Jerold Apps, *The Adult Learner On Campus* (Chicago, IL: Follett Publishing Company, 1981) page 156.

[2]Jane Vella, *Training Through Dialogue* (San Francisco, CA: Jossey-Bass Publishers, 1995), page 16.

[3]Apps, Page 154.

[4]Robert M Smith and Associates, *Learning to Learn Across the Life Span* (San Francisco, CA: Jossey-Bass Publishers, 1991), pagers 125-129.

[5]Vella, page 36.

[6]Ralph Ruddock, "All Right on the Night- A Survival Kit for Absolute Beginners," *Adult Education* (London), Volume 45, Number 3, 1972, page 145.

Chapter 10

[1]Brookfield, page 75.

[2]Nelson, page 14.

[3]Eble, pages 52-53.

[4]Brookfield, page 204.

[5]Eble, page 60.

Chapter 11

[1]Chapter 11 consists of excerpts and summaries of concepts from *Energizing the Learning Environment,* by William A. Draves (Manhattan, KS: Learning Resources Network, 1995).

[2]The Lind Institute, P.O. Box 14487, San Francisco, CA.

Chapter 12

[1]Verduin, et al, page 24.

[2]Glen Ramsborg, *Objectives to Outcomes; Your Contract with the Learner* (Birmingham, AL: Professional Convention Man agement Association, 1993), page 57.

Rita-Marie Conrad and J. Ana Donaldson, *Engaging the Online Learner,* (San Francisco, Jossey-Bass, 2004).

[3]Robinson, page 78.

[4]Ibid.

[5]H.R. Mills, Teaching and Training: A Handbook for Instructors (New York, NY: John Wiley & Sons, 1977), page 97.

[6]Kenneth Eble, The Craft of Teaching, second edition (San Francisco, CA: Jossey-Bass Publishers, 1988), page 148.

[7]Waynne James and Phil Offill, Idea Book for Designing More Effective Learning Activities (Stillwater, OK: Oklahoma State University, 1979), pages 143-144.

Chapter 13

[1]Draves, Course Evaluations (Manhattan, KS: Learning Resources Network, 1980), pages 1-4

[2]Ibid.

[3]Robinson, page 102

Chapter 14

[1]*Generational Learning Styles,* by Julie Coates, Learning Resources Network, 2007.

[2]Laura Taylor interview with Julie Coates, Raleigh, NC, November 2005.

[3]For example, instructor Sharon Summer reports using boys to help in some of her workshops. She reported, "Students teaching the teacher worked then, and many, many times through the years. They love teaching and they will love teaching you." Sharon Summer, Missouri Baptist University, St. Louis, MO, in "Advanced Teaching Online" course, August 23, 2010.

[4]See the chapter N-Gen Learning in *Growing Up Digital: The Rise of the Net Generation,* by Don Tapscott, McGraw-Hill, 1998.

[5]*Using Learning Contracts: Practical Approaches to Individualizing and*

Structuring Learning, by Malcolm Knowles, Jossey-Bass Publishers, San Francisco, 1986.

[6]"Failure not an option: Ontario students can try, try again," by Joanne Laucius, Canwest News Service, May 11, 2009.

Chapter 16

[1]*Boys and Girls Learn Differently,* by Michael Gurian, Jossey Bass, 2010

[2]*The Essential Difference,* Simon Baron-Cohen, Basic Books, 2003

[3]*Sex and Cognition,* by Doreen Kimura, MIT Press, 2000

[4]*Gender and Fair Assessment,* Warren Willingham and Nancy S. Cole, Educational Testing Service, Lawrence Earlbaum Associates, 1997

Chapter 17

[1]*Gender and Fair Assessment,* Warren Willingham and Nancy S. Cole, Educational Testing Service, Lawrence Earlbaum Associates, 1997

[2]The Reversal of Gender Inequalities in Higher Education: An On-going Trend, by Stéphan Vincent-Lancrin, Higher Education to 2030, OECD, 2008, ISBN 978-92-64-04065-6.

[3]*Academically Adrift, by Richard Arum,* University of Chicago Press, 2011.

[4]Mike Baker, BBC Education Correspondent, 2007.

Online Courses for Your Further Professional Development

From the Learning Resources Network, the leading provider of online professional development for teachers.

Check www.TeachingOntheNet.org or UGotClass.net for next offerings and additional information.

- Certificate in Teaching Adults
- Advanced Teaching Online
- Gender in the Classroom
- Students with Asperger's
- Certified Online Instructor (COI)
- Fostering Online Discussion
- Using Cell Phones in the Classroom
- Designing Hybrid Courses
  and more....

About the Author

William A. Draves is an internationally recognized teacher, author and consultant, and one of the foremost authorities on adult learning.

He is President of the Learning Resources Network (LERN), the world's leading association in lifelong learning with more than 5,000 members.

Draves is the most-quoted expert on lifelong learning by the nation's media, having been interviewed by The New York Times, BBC, Washington Post, Wall Street Journal, National Public Radio, NBC Nightly News, and Wired.com, among others.

He holds a master's degree in adult education from The George Washington University in Washington, DC. With co-author Julie Coates he has also written *Education in the 21st Century,* and their classic work *Nine Shift: Work, Life and Education in the 21st Century.* He is also author of *Advanced Teaching Online* and well as *Energizing the Learning Environment.*

A popular speaker, he has keynoted conferences in Russia, Japan, Australia, England, Slovenia, and throughout Canada and the United States.

Speaking Availability

"A world-class speaker."
— Maureen Geddes, Vice President, Ontario Speakers Association

"So good I started applauding half-way through."
— Dr. Janet K. Lewis, Office of the Executive Director,
South Dakota Board of Regents, Pierre, SD

"I'd trample my grandma to hear Draves speak."
— Phil Houseal, Kerrville, Texas

For your next conference or meeting, invite one of the world's foremost authorities on teaching adults, lifelong learning and life in the 21st century.

William A. Draves has keynoted conferences, conducted seminars, and done presentations all over the world, including Japan, Russia, Australia, Germany, United Kingdom, Mexico, Slovenia and around the United States.

Mr. Draves is available for:

- Conference keynotes
- Consulting
- Seminars
  - In-house training
  - On-site workshops
- Interviews
  and more...

Presentations can be customized to your audience and situation.

For information and availability, email Mr. Draves at draves@lern.org